Testament of Memory

Testament of Memory

A Siberian Life

Mikhail Vasilievich Chevalkov

This is a translation of a text originally published by the
Gorno-Altai section of the Altai Publishing House in 1990
with an introduction by Brontoi Ya. Bedyurov.

Translation and short introduction by Dr. John Warden

Holy Trinity Publications
The Printshop of St Job of Pochaev
Holy Trinity Monastery
Jordanville, New York
2011

Printed with the blessing of His Eminence,
Metropolitan Hilarion, First Hierarch
of the Russian Orthodox Church Outside of Russia

HOLY TRINITY PUBLICATIONS
The Printshop of St Job of Pochaev
Holy Trinity Monastery
Jordanville, New York 13361-0036
www.holytrinitypublications.com

ISBN 978-0-88465-184-0 (Paperback)
ISBN 978-0-88465-204-5 (ePub)

Library of Congress Control 2010940794

THE ALTAI REPUBLIC TODAY

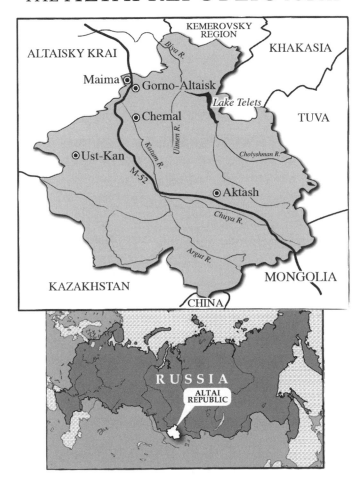

CONTENTS

Introduction   ix

1. **A Journey Begins**   1
   Awakening to God   3
   The Wisdom of Father Macarios   18
   A New Home   28

2. **Interpreter of Faith**   33
   On Missionary Roads   43
   Baptism of Tiban   53
   Prayers Answered by St Nicholas   60
   Pagan Ways   69

3. **Raising Voices and Hearts to God**   77
   A Women's Monastery   83
   Russian Emissary to China   90
   Baptizing among the Yurts   103
   Miracles Never Cease   117
   The Baptism of the People of Ak-Korymsk   128

4. **Admonitions to My Children**   135
   To My Children and Their Descendants   135
   The Long Arm   136
   My Children!   139

Index   141

Archpriest Mikhail Vasilievich Chevalkov

INTRODUCTION

This small work by M. V. Chevalkov (1817–1901) has several claims to the attention of the English-speaking reader. It is rare to encounter a text about which we could use the word "modest" in such a truly affirmative sense. The style is simple, direct, and unpretentious, yet at the same time it is always interesting, even fascinating, to read. The author himself was a man of great moral courage and integrity but also a man of great humility and modesty. He was a fine example of the virtues demanded by the religion he professed.

There are three reasons why the autobiography of this most modest man must be regarded as especially valuable: It provides us with a unique picture of the life of the people of the High Altai region of the Russian Empire in the mid-nineteenth century; it gives us an intimate account of the missionary work of the Russian Orthodox Church in the region at the time; and, finally, it is most notable as the first "literary" work written in the Altai language. Chevalkov was a pioneer both in his missionary work and in the establishment of the Altai language as a vehicle for literature.

The High Altai region is situated just within the Russian Empire (later USSR) on the borders of Mongolia and the Chinese province of Sinkiang in the east, Kazakhstan to the south, and southwestern Siberia to the north and west. It is an extremely mountainous region, with mountains rising to over 10,000 feet, deep river valleys, and lakes. The climate is extreme, as we would expect in an area of southern Siberia at the heart of the Eurasian landmass. In the mid-nineteenth century, the boundaries between Russia and China were in dispute in many areas, and Chevalkov describes one such small-scale boundary dispute between Russia and China in which he became involved and stoutly defended the Russian position. In short, the High Altai region was one of the most far-flung remote corners of the vast Russian Empire, little known to outsiders until the 1860s when scholars such as Vasilii Vasilevitch Radlov began to explore the area and study the local languages and cultures.

Part of Chevalkov's work was first published by Radlov in an anthology of studies of the Altai region in 1864. The autobiography was expanded and published as a second edition in 1894. The whole work—both the first and the expanded later edition—gives us a quite detailed picture of the life and culture of the native peoples of the area. It is most important to note that this is not the picture or impressions of an outsider but the picture given by a native Altai whose work and travels as a missionary took him all over the region. Unlike western "orientalists" such as Radlov, Chevalkov knew Altai life with an intimacy possessed only by a native whose first language was local and whose parents and family were originally pagans and followed the traditional way of life. This is what makes the autobiography so valuable. It is a picture of the life of the High Altai in the middle of the nineteenth century when many of the old ways and practices still survived.

Chevalkov was married at sixteen according to custom and illiterate until his late teens, when he largely taught himself and learned Russian. He had no formal education and yet became invaluable as a translator not only to the missionaries but also to the orientalists (such as Radlov) who began to study his people in the 1860s. This lack of formal education adds to the charm of his work, which does not suffer from the limitations of scholarly works about the region that were inhibited about including minor details that Chevalkov describes on the assumption that all will be of interest. His work is indeed very personal: It is a view of the people and society around him through the eyes and ears of Chevalkov himself. He does indeed have a point of view—that conversion to Orthodox Christianity was highly desirable for his people—and he worked for sixty years to this end.

He did not, however, have any sociological perspectives or scientific preconceptions, which would have weakened the immediacy of his accounts. He simply describes Altai life as it was. He was often poor, and even later when he was well known he was often short of funds for his family. He was certainly not a member of the intelligentsia or middle class and therefore never detached from the life of the people he describes. The time of his original work (1864) also coincides with the first penetration of the area by Russian settlers who were introducing a Russian or European style of life. Chevalkov's description of the High Altai was therefore just in time, for within fifty years European styles had begun to produce irrevocable changes, and many aspects of the life described in the autobiography had become very rare or even extinct.

The second valuable aspect of the autobiography is the glimpse it gives of the missionary work that the Russian Orthodox Church was undertaking in the area at this time. In most western books about Christian missions, there is very little reference to the Orthodox Church as a great missionary church. In fact the opposite is the case. As early as the sixteenth century the Russian church, through the monastic establishments it encouraged, took Christianity first to the northwest beyond Perm and then to the Ural Mountains into Siberia and beyond. In the eastern territories of the empire, the church was a missionary church, and it sought to convert the native peoples as well as provide for Russian settlers. An interesting example of this exists to this day in Alaska, which was Russian until 1867. There, many of the native peoples are still Orthodox, as they have been since the missions in the eighteenth and nineteenth centuries. The members of non-Orthodox churches are primarily settlers from the mainland United States and their descendants.

The High Altai regions in the mid-nineteenth century were still "pagan," and we may describe their religion as shamanism. In the past, there had been waves of various cultural influences: from the Chinese came Buddhism and Taoism, whereas the Turkic peoples to the south spread Islamic ideas and perhaps even Manicheanism and Nestorianism. Nevertheless, these influences were weak, and the main religion was shamanism. The Russian Orthodox mission to the area was founded by Father Macarios (Glukharev) in 1828. He settled in Biysk as permanent priest in residence in 1830. He was a considerable influence upon the young Chevalkov. The missionaries, especially those who were sympathetic to the Altai native peoples (which was mostly the case), made a fundamental contribution to the work of establishing a written Altai culture based upon the use of the Russian alphabet and the creation of a literary language. In addition, the missionaries gave invaluable service in creating the first scientific and practical grammar of the Altai language, which became a classic of its type. Later, following this model, the grammars of many other Turkic languages were to be defined. Archimandrite Macarios introduced a version of the Bible in the Altai language in the late 1830s. It is amazing to think that this work was begun in 1837 on Easter, not somewhere in highly educated Orthodox centers in the West but far on the frontiers in pagan Altai, in a small place called Ulala! The key to this translation was the work of the young Chevalkov, the newly literate native working with Father Macarios. This is described in his autobiography.

Father Macarios was certainly an exceptional figure. He was a well-educated theologian who had command of several languages, including Greek and Hebrew. He translated the Bible into modern Russian. In his early years he studied the philosophy of the German philosopher Johann Gottfried von Herder, was also familiar with the botanical work of Linnaeus and Denandel and the works of the astronomer John Herschel, and in general took a great interest in the natural sciences. For some time, he was a professor at the Theological Academy in Kostroma. From contemporary descriptions he seems to have been a man of great holiness who gave incorruptible service and love to the native peoples. In his approach to his missionary work, he advocated a definite program: It was not only to baptize the "natives" and turn them into true citizens of the heavenly kingdom but also to lead them to a settled way of life, to guide them to literacy, and to encourage them toward a more developed and more profitable form of agricultural practice. His program demanded of the missionaries a thorough knowledge of the Altai language, some basic ideas of science and medicine, and an understanding of agrarian economics. He prepared for the mission such practically useful objects as seeds for market gardening and fruit growing, agricultural tools, and so on. He produced the first translation into Altai of prayers and texts for church services. For the first time in the history of the missionary movement, he took seriously the organization of missionary activities for women. He appointed female assistants. The first among these were the Russian Praskovia Landysheva and the Frenchwoman Sofia Belmont. Among their duties were the education of the newly converted Altai women in the skills of child care, sewing, bread making, elementary medical care, and the fundamentals of midwifery. He even established an icon-painting studio where some gifted students learned about the fine arts to the extent that in time they launched the Altai school of painting, which spread over the whole region.

Clearly the mission established in 1828 by Father Macarios was highly significant in the development of the region in the nineteenth century. Its founder was a remarkable man, and we meet him through Chevalkov. In a way, we may say that Chevalkov carried further the work of Father Macarios, who left the region in the 1840s on health grounds, as described in the autobiography. Through Chevalkov's little book we travel with a missionary, overhear his conversations with the pagans, and see the gradual expansion in the numbers of the Orthodox faithful. We see the man himself as a young convert who later becomes a deacon and then priest and never loses his humility even when his name had become well known beyond the Altai.

When we refer to the publication in the 1840s of prayer books, religious songs, service books, and the Bible itself in the Altai language, we are, of course, referring to the translation work of Mikhail Chevalkov. In many languages, the first use of the vernacular was in such works. This was certainly true of Russian itself, which was first used in translations of a similar type and also notably in sermons given in Russian in the eleventh century. Chevalkov the translator was therefore a pioneer in the creation and use of the Altai vernacular. His autobiography, titled in Altai *Undulbas kerees*, written after encouragement by Radlov, was first published in the latter's anthology *Samples of the National Literatures of the Turkic Peoples* in 1864. Later Chevalkov wrote a book of parables and poems. During his life, his works were published in St Petersburg in 1866, Kazan in 1872 and 1881, Tomsk in 1883, and Moscow in 1894. The publication of the autobiography in 1894 was in the Moscow missionary journal *Orthodox News* (No. 5), and later it appeared as a separate book. It was translated by Macarios Nevsky. The version of 1894 (which is the version translated here) was an expansion by Chevalkov of the version of the 1860s. Neither the *Testament of Memory* nor his allegorical poems, verse, parables, and maxims exhaust the total of his literary achievement. There is also the wide range of translation work by Chevalkov: His arrangements and adaptations of stories from holy Scripture are of enormous artistic, literary, and philological interest. In his usual modest way, Chevalkov does not appear to have been aware that he was making literary history by his use of the Altai language to compose these works, and yet he could certainly be seen as one of the main and perhaps most important creators of the Altai literary language.

'The text translated here is from the version published by the Gorno-Altai section of the Altai Book Publishing House in 1990. This was approved for publication in November 1989. These dates are of more than passing interest. It must be kept in mind that M. S. Gorbachev assumed office in 1985, and by the late 1980s his policy of *glasnost* (allowing more freedom of speech) was beginning to have an impact upon publishing in the USSR. Before that date, the possibility of publishing a work by an Orthodox missionary such as Chevalkov, however important in the context of the history of the Altai region, was out of the question. In the 1920s and 1930s, during the time of militant atheism, religion and any respect for it was attacked mercilessly. Therefore, any publishing house or editor would avoid figures such as Chevalkov for fear of being ridiculed and regarded with great suspicion. From the 1940s until the late 1980s, religion was officially regarded as, by definition, backward, primitive, and of no interest to the educated person. Consequently, any works by believers such as Chevalkov remained in the sphere of interest of specialist scholars who could claim their references to such works were purely for academic and scholarly reasons. Missionaries and their works were, of course, still to be regarded as backward and unscientific, but their writings and memoirs could be used to throw light upon the social history of their time.

At last, after 1985, such attitudes began to change, and works by major Russian Orthodox philosophers, never before published in the USSR, began to be published and become widely known there. This edition of the autobiography of Chevalkov must be seen in this context. There is no question that the writer was an Orthodox Christian believer, and the book shows the man and his beliefs in a very positive and sympathetic light. The edition of 1990 has a long and excellent introduction by Brontoi Ya. Bedyurov. In this the writer himself pours scorn upon the dogmatically atheistic attitude of the previous period that precluded any serious appreciation of the work of Chevalkov. He gives an objective appraisal, for example, of the role of the missions in Altai and describes Father Macarios in a very positive light. Bedyurov's introduction gives full praise to Chevalkov and his achievements and takes great pride in his role in the High Altai in the nineteenth century. Quite simply, the work translated here could not have appeared in the USSR in 1980, but in 1989 the scholar Bedyurov and his colleagues were able to offer

it to Russian readers with obvious enthusiastic approval
and admiration for the author and his work.

Dr. John Warden

Retired lecturer in Russian and Soviet Studies at the
University of Coventry in Central England

CHAPTER I

A Journey Begins

My daughters: Matryona, Maria, and Yelena! I am giving to the three of you a description of my life, as my testament for you and your children in memory of me.

My children! I come from the Mundusov family, of the White Telyeutov clan: my father's name was Andrash; Andrash's father was Kilyemyesh, and his father was Semyeek; Semyeek's father was Soyogosh, and his father was Sepyerek; and the father of Sepyerek was Chebelek. We Chevalkovs, who now live in Ulala and Bachat, descended from him. My mother's name was Kabrozh, and her father was called Kulbes. This Kulbes was a leader among his people; he was of the Tyuuty family, of the Kyshtymsky clan. I, one of their descendants, was of the "dark faith" (paganism) until my seventeenth year. My father and mother gave me the Christian name Kiprian (people who live near Russians, although they are pagans, quite often give their children Christian names).

There you are, children; I have written about my ancestors so that you will not forget them!

Now I will tell you what my elders told me about our ancestors' history. In the old days there was Terbet, the Oirotsky khan who ruled four clans. This was when sixty *tyumen* (lowlanders) of the Telyeutov clan of the Golden Horde lived at peace together. After this, there was a dispute among the four clans, and they began to fight among themselves. Because of this, the Oirotsky khan went away to live in the land of the Kunkersky khan. Those sultans and headmen who remained gathered their followers together and dispersed themselves into various lands, seeking a peaceful place to settle. A minority of the people who were left lived on both sides of the river Irtysh.

The Telyeuty lived on both banks of the river Ak-Umara (Obi), but they did not live in peace with one another. As a result of constant warfare, their numbers seriously declined and they were constantly troubled on one hand by the Mongols led by Chudak and on the other by the "Dark Kirgiz" (Kara Kazak). When my ancestor Sepyerek, son of Chebelek, was alive, our forefathers voluntarily became subjects of the "White Tsar" in Russia and began to pay *alman* (tribute).[1] The Telyeuty, led

---

[1] The Telyeutians were a southern Altain tribe who submitted to Russian rule in 1756 during the reign of the Empress Elizabeth (1741–1761). By the end of the century, they were paying tribute to the Russian Tsar Paul (1796–1801).

by the tribal chiefs Mamyt and Balyk, came to the town of Kuznetsk and made a request to the *tyorye-bii* (governor of the town) in the following terms: "We are willing to pay tribute to the White Tsar so that we may live under his protection in this land."

My father was born in Bachat. When my father was ten years old, his parents and his brothers moved to and settled in a small place called Karasu, which is now the village of Karasuk, not far from the town of Biysk. There were five brothers: the oldest, Kalan; then Yegor; then, younger than he, my father, Andrash; younger than he was Ustepko; and then Yaras. Their father was Kilyemyesh and their mother was Keyelesh. Here, Andrash grew up, married Kabrozh, and started his own family.

AWAKENING TO GOD

When I was seven years old, my parents moved from there to live in Ulala. Together with us were four households. After two years, a certain Afanasii Konshin settled in Ulala with his wife and three children. They were townspeople. This townsman had a son, Yakov, who was the same age as I was, and I played with him and learned the Russian language. At his home before eating a meal, Yakov would always say a prayer, having turned first toward the opposite corner. He prayed in the same way after the meal. Amazed at this, I asked him, "Why do you pray before and after a meal?" He answered, "Before eating a meal we ask for God's blessing, and after eating the meal we give God thanks." Hearing this and seeing how pleasing this habit must be to God, I became dissatisfied with my own ways and said to myself, "When you want to eat, you do not ask for God's blessing, and when you have eaten your fill, you do not give any thanks to God. You eat up and then go off like a dog, not giving any thought to God, who gives you your food." In my heart, I was ashamed of myself that our faith was not very good. I was then nine years old.

Once, on another occasion, Yakov and I went to the place where his family had their beehive. After we played for awhile, we lay on our backs and gazed into the sky. I asked Yakov, "What is up there in the sky?" He answered, "God is there." Next, I asked him, "What is this God called?" Yakov replied, "Jesus Christ. He created all the people who are on the earth, all kinds of livestock, wild animals, and birds. Now He is in Heaven." I asked, "Does this God see us from there?" He answered, "He sees us and all that we do, day and night. He loves those people who pray to Him, and He does not like those who do not pray." Then I asked him one more question: "What does He do with those people He does not like?" He said, "I heard from my mother that He sends those people whom He does not like into fire and darkness."

After this, I began to feel ashamed in my heart and also guilty. When my parents were practicing shamanism (offering sacrifices) and some Russians came to see us, I was very ashamed in front of them. When my father sent me to look after the cows, I sometimes climbed the Tugai (Uttu-Kai) and sat on a stone where *badan* [a kind of grass that was used in place of tea—Ed.] was growing. Turning my face to the east, I bowed down and said the name of Jesus Christ. I bowed down but did not know what prayers I should say, so I only kept repeating several times, "God, Jesus Christ, do not leave me but take me to Yourself!"

My children! Even now from far away, that place seems so beautiful to me, and to this day it has not disappeared from my memory.

I remember something else: One day, I went to my friend Yakov's house, and while I was sitting there, in came three men dressed in black, wearing flat black hats on their heads. I wanted to run away, but one of them stopped me, asked me to sit down beside him, and gave me a red currant tart. I sat there thinking, shall I eat it or not? Looking straight at me, the man asked me my name. "Kiprian," I answered. He said, "I will tell you a story, and you sit there comfortably and listen." Placing his hand on my shoulder, he said, "In the old days, there was a great chief, Kiprian, who went up into the mountains to learn about demons and the black arts. Once he had learned all this, he could do whatever he wanted, but one thing he could not do. He could not overcome a baptized girl called Istina with his demonic spells. Amazed at this, he asked one of the chief demons who served him, 'Up to this time you have been able to do whatever you wanted: how come now you cannot overcome this girl?' His servants said to him, 'We are afraid of her God, so we cannot approach either her or her house.' When he heard this, he went up to the girl and asked, 'What God do you believe in?' Istina told him about Jesus Christ. After this, Kiprian was baptized, became a great priest, and by God's grace performed many miracles. Now, after his death, he lives in eternal bliss, in the light of God."

After hearing this story, I asked, "Who are you? What is your name?" Smiling, he told me he was a priest called Macarios. "You should be baptized, and you will become one of God's servants. The unbaptized never see God's light but will spend their time with the devil and go into the darkness and fire from which they can never escape," he said. Then he told me about those who believe in God and those who do not believe. Hearing all that he said, I could hardly control my tears. I would have liked to be baptized but was afraid of my parents. I was then eleven years old.

When I had passed my twelfth birthday and was in my thirteenth year, my parents arranged my betrothal to a girl. In the same year, my mother died of a fever. After the death of my beloved mother, I very rarely laughed and wept much more frequently. In this way I passed two years with much weeping. During these years, I looked after the cows by myself, washed all the linen, and prepared all the meals. In the third year, my father married me off to the girl to whom I had been betrothed.

I was then sixteen years old. At this time, the people who lived in Ulala began to seek baptism. When, along with our family, two other families did not wish to be baptized, Father Macarios said, "You, the unbaptized, if you practice shamanism while living among the baptized, you will be a temptation to them. For this reason, if you do not want to be baptized, you should return to your own place, Kuznetsk." Therefore, my father handed over my wife and myself to the oversight of my father-in-law and my father left for Bachat. We, too, set out on our way, and when we began to leave our native place, I could not hold back my tears. On the third day, when we could no longer see the Altai hills and started to cross the steppe lands, I thought to myself, "Why weren't you baptized? Why, not fearing the God in Heaven but fearing your earthly father, are you moving to Bachat?"

One day in the spring of the year after we arrived in Bachat, I was sitting on Mount Elbai, and my heart was very sad. At that moment, Kaimak, son of Orgon, came up to me and said, "From this place, Shanda, it is ten *versts* (six miles) to the Bachat district center, and there is a church there. Tomorrow, a lot of people will gather there for the Feast of Mikola (St Nicholas). Are you going?" I said, "I do not know the way, but I would like to go." Kaimak said, "A lot of people will be going there from Shanda; perhaps you could travel with them."

I was overjoyed and saddled my horse. Many women were going, and I went with them, but I could not keep up because my horse was not very good. So I arrived in Bachat on my own and did not know anyone there with whom I could stay. I rode down the street alone with tears in my eyes. Then I met my uncle Chenosh from Bolshoi Ulus, and he said, "Kinsman, have you come for the feast?" I replied, "Yes, for the feast." He then went on with me. We came to the house of a peasant, Klemeshev, and the two of us stayed with him.

There was a great ringing of bells, and I asked my uncle, "What is that?" "They are ringing the bell so that the people can gather in the church," he answered. (Up to this time I had never seen a church.) So my uncle and I went to the church. On our way, a strange fellow walked beside us. On the top of his hat, he had paper tassels; he was wearing a frock coat, and on his shoulders he had paper flowers. When I saw him, I asked my uncle, "Is this an *abyz* (priest)?" My uncle said, "This is Yevsei, the fool." I asked, "And has he done anyone any harm?" My uncle answered, "No, he has never done any harm to anyone." So Yevsei went along to the church with us, and after we entered, he stood by the doors with us. When we were praying, he often looked at me and smiled. The people standing in front of me were taller than I was, so I could not see what was happening in front. The unbaptized Telyeut people standing near me bowed but did not make the sign of the cross upon themselves, although they did pray. I could hear from the front of the church a large number of people singing and praising God. The pleasure of this singing brought tears to my eyes.

When we had left the church, my uncle and I went back to the flat, where we had lunch. Afterward, my uncle said to me, "Kinsman, why do you stand with your head so bowed? What makes you so sad?" "I am bored in a strange land." He said, "The chief of our Telyeut clan is here, and he is a good man. Let's go to him; he has an organ, and he will play something on it for us." So we set out. When we arrived, the man led us into the upper room and asked my uncle, "Whose son is this?" My uncle answered, "He is my kinsman; he has come from the Altai." The chief answered, "He should be taught how to read and write," and my uncle replied, "He is missing his home; play something for him." The man began to play the organ. I listened but became even more sad and wept. Afterward, the chief entertained us with tea and poured two glasses of wine for my uncle. From his place, we returned home.

Remembering my homeland, I said to myself, "Why did you move to the Bachat district instead of accepting this faith where there is such beautiful singing?" I was so sad and wept. My mother-in-law, seeing my tears, said, "What are you so sad and miserable about my son? Doesn't your wife show you respect? You tell me." I said, "No, she doesn't treat me wrongly; I am always thinking of my homeland." My mother-in-law said, "In the autumn we will go to stay in Ulala, and soon your father is coming here."

From such depression I fell ill and lay in bed for about a week. When I was lying in bed ill, my father came into the house, dressed in a white shirt and black hat. When I saw him, I burst into tears. My father said, "Why are you crying, my son?" I said, "You settle down to live here, but I am going back to Ulala to be baptized." My father, seeing me weeping, himself burst into tears and said, "If you wanted to be baptized, my son, why didn't you tell us then?" I answered, "I was afraid to speak to you about it." My mother-in-law responded, "I will take my daughter back," and I replied, "If you want to take her, then you know best."

A week later, we set out to return to Ulala. Many of our relatives who had come to bid us farewell wept over us as if we were dead. "You, Andrash," they said, "have listened to your young son: you are going away to be baptized, so you are now no longer of our family." I found it unpleasant to hear their lamentations, but we set out and within five days arrived in Ulala.

We were baptized in the autumn of that year. I was given the name Mikhail and my father Vasilii; my wife was named Alexandra; my younger sister became Yelena and the youngest of all, Maria. I also had a brother Erok, younger than I by seven years. When he was only two months old, he was given by my father for adoption to his older brother, who had no children. When he was ten years old, he was sent to learn to read and write. He was now called Andrian because my uncle's family had been baptized before us.

The house of Mikhail Ashchaulov was on the left bank of the river Ulala. Father Macarios bought it and lived there. We lived on the right bank of the Ulala. My brother often went to Father Macarios to learn to read and write. Seeing that he was learning this, I was upset and said to myself, "My younger brother will have learned to read; he will be familiar with the word of God and understand right from wrong. And now I will be worse and more stupid than the rest." I was depressed about this and prayed, "My Lord God, Jesus Christ, Thy will be done! If my wish to learn to read and write is acceptable to Thee, then open my mind and teach me Thyself!"

Once, when I had finished feeding the animals, I went to see Father Macarios, and he told me things about God. I listened, and what he told me was sweeter than honey to me. His words imprinted themselves directly into my heart. From that time, just like a bee who has found honey, every evening I went to see Father Macarios. Often when I was visiting Father Macarios, I asked the holy men who lived with him if they would teach me to read and write. They answered, "You come to us in the daytime, and we will teach you with your brother." So I went to study for two days in a row.

My father asked me, "Where are you going?" I answered, "I am going to Father Macarios to learn to read and write." My father replied angrily, "That's enough if your younger brother learns, but you should get on with your own business. Reading and writing is for lazy people, and you are too lazy to work. People are laughing at you, and in fact two men said to me, 'You are teaching your son to be lazy. See? He is going to the *abyz* to learn to read and write.'" After this, keeping it secret from my father and my wife, I went to the store-room and wept.

Later, I said to my brother, Andrian, "When you come to have dinner, bring your alphabet book with you." Andrian did this, and when he came home to dinner, he read the alphabet for me. When I, sitting silently by his side, studied the alphabet with him, my father said, "What are you sitting around for? You do not do any work but ruin your eyes." But after I finished my work, I listened to Andrian read aloud. Just as you learn a song, so in the same way I learned to read the alphabet by ear. When my father was not at home, I looked over the words and recognized them, at the same time asking my brother for explanations. However, I was not able to make out all the words.

One time, the foreman came and ordered me to take Father Macarios to the valley of Maima. I harnessed two horses and went to Father Macarios's house; when I got there, Father Macarios was tying about thirty primers into a bundle. I asked him, "Father Macarios! Be so good as to give me a primer!" Father Macarios smiled, came up to me, and said, "You are a married family man: do you have enough free time to learn to read?" I answered, "If God helps me, I will learn." Father Macarios took one primer and said, "If you can make out three words in this primer, then I will give it to you with my blessing, but if you cannot do so, I will not give it to you at this time." Although I could not recognize many of the words, from memory I repeated what the primer said as well as I could. Once he had heard this, Father Macarios asked me, "Who taught you?" I answered that no one had taught me. I taught myself while Andrian read the primer aloud and I got on with my work and listened and learned. Father Macarios said, "Do not say you taught yourself; if God does not help, then man cannot do anything by himself and cannot teach himself anything. When you want to do something, say, 'Lord Jesus Christ, Thy will be done! If it pleases Thee that I should begin this work, then give it Thy blessing.' Then if God is pleased with what you want to do, He will certainly help you with it. But ask God's blessing in faith, and when you have asked, you will find that God will certainly give it, and if your request has been answered by God, then do not think in your heart, 'I did this myself.' If you start thinking that you have done this all by yourself, then the devil will plunder the seeds of your good deeds like a bird stealing the seed of wheat."

Having admonished me in this way, he placed his hand upon my head and stood there silently. Then he gave me the primer, which I received with great joy and hid under my shirt. When I had loaded the things onto the cart, Father Macarios came out, sat down, and said, "Take me to Maima." Until we reached Maima, he taught me. When I got home, I hid the primer in the barn. After that, when I set out for work, I took the primer with me, and on the road I taught myself to understand the words. If I noticed that someone was coming toward me, then I hid my primer under my shirt; when he had passed by, I began my studies again. Sometimes I asked my brother for help and sometimes, in secret from my father, I went out to Father Macarios's place and studied with his assistants.

One evening, I went to Father Macarios's house. When I arrived, Father Macarios came out and asked, "Well, have you learned to read and write?" I answered, "Glory be to God! I know a bit." He brought out a copy of the Old Testament and asked me to read some of it to him. I read five lines. He turned his gaze toward the heavens and said, "Blessed art Thou, O Lord of Zion, who hath created Heaven and earth!" When he had said that, he gave the book to me. Then he took me by the hand, led me to a chair, and asked me to sit down. He sat down near me and began to teach me the word of God. He said, "Whoever bears affliction with patience will find that which is sweet; whoever weeps will rejoice. Do not be upset that people offend you; do not harbor hate toward those who do evil to you and cause you tears. For us sinners, the Lord came down from Heaven to earth and bore for our sakes the sufferings of the cross but did not seek vengeance upon those who tortured Him. For our God, Jesus Christ, by His sufferings and His own blood, redeemed us from eternal death and eternal fire. Whoever, for God's sake, bears insult patiently will in this godlike way gain His blessing." He said also, "Whoever loses his soul for God's sake will find it truly." Having listened to these words, the sweetest honey to me, I returned home feeling as you do after a good meal.

When I got home, my father said, "Where have you been?" I took the book from my bag and showing it to him said, "I was at Father Macarios's; he gave me this book and told me to study it." My father said, "Well, then, read some of it." I began to read it to him with some hesitation. My father, once he had heard me, said, "Well, if you already know so much, then go ahead and feel free to study." From these words I became bright and joyful in my soul, like when a bright fire lights up a dark night or the sun shines through on a dull day. Receiving such a blessing from my father gave me great joy.

I began to go in the evenings, after feeding the cattle, to Father Macarios's assistants in order to pursue my studies. When they did not have any time free for me, I returned home after waiting there for a short time in vain. While I waited there, a widowed priest called Father Vasilii often said to me, "Haven't you got anything to do at home as you seem to spend so much time here?" On hearing these remarks I returned home in tears, saying to myself, I must be a very unfortunate person to find myself faced with so many obstacles.

Again one day I came to Father Macarios. He was drinking tea at the time, and I went up to him, received his blessing, and then withdrew and stood by the door. Father Macarios said, "Sit down there on the chair." I bowed and then sat down, and he poured me some tea, which I began to drink. He asked me, "How are things? Are you getting on alright?" I said, "Glory be to God, all is well." He then further questioned me, "Do you say your prayers to God in the morning?" "Indeed, I do pray," I answered. "So you do indeed pray. But that might mean you pray in a lazy way. Don't just pray; go deep into your heart and pray there in secret. When you can pray like that, then the Heavenly Father will really give you the Kingdom of Heaven; when you pray, stand with fear as if you really can see God before you and, saying your prayers in this way, say, 'My God, Jesus Christ, save me, a sinner! I have committed many sins before Thy face; save me! Invisible to me, Thou seest all of me, and Thou knowest the thoughts of my heart!'" After this he got up, took into his hands a copy of the Gospels, and, standing before me, said, "In this book are written the life story of God Himself and His teachings, and also the actions and teachings of His disciples. Every day you must read one chapter from this. If you read this with faith, then you will be the same as those who heard the words from the mouth of God Himself." When he had said this, he blessed me with the sign of the cross, held out the book for me to kiss, and gave it to me.

Having received this gift, I returned home full of a great joy and lightness of heart, as if I had found a brilliant precious stone. The book was written in two languages: on one side in Russian and on the other in Slavic. I showed the book to my father. My father said, "If you have the ability to understand the word of God, then through this book you can teach others, but if you do not, then it will be lying about in this house in vain. Now pray to God. May God help you!"

May the Lord, who created Heaven and earth, give His blessing and light to Father Macarios, through whom I have acquired great joy and blessing, like a bird gathering grain. By his encouragement in learning the ways of God, I passed my days in great happiness. Sometimes in my heart I began to forget the kindness of God's actions toward me. Then, like a bird that has exhausted all the grain it had gathered for its food, I made my way to Father Macarios and he again fed me, calmed me, and warmed me with the words of God. And so in the course of three years I went to Father Macarios, like a bee that has found itself a ready supply of honey. Sometimes, when I was doing something that was contrary to God's will, Father Macarios would cause me to weep and fall upon my knees in prayer to God. May God give him light and blessing! He taught me nothing harmful but only things good and profitable for my soul.

THE WISDOM OF FATHER MACARIOS

One day when I went to Father Macarios's place, Osip Naurchakov and Pavel Surochakov were with him. When he saw me, Father Macarios came over and, having given me his blessing, asked me to sit down. The three of them were translating the story of Joseph (Gen 37–50), and I sat down to one side. In translating this story into the Altai language, they were having difficulty with the Russian word *ibo* [because—Ed.]. Father Macarios asked me, "How would you translate *ibo*?" I answered, "Give me an example." He gave me an example, and I said, "In our language that means *teze*." Father Macarios called his servant, Stepan Vasilievich, and said, "Light the samovar. We will drink tea to celebrate now that we have found the long sought-after word!" After this, Father Macarios said to me, "When you are free, come to me, and the two of us will translate the life of Joseph. This will be useful for you, and you will be studying the holy Scriptures." So in my free time, I went to Father Macarios's until we had finished the translation of the life of Joseph. After we finished, Father Macarios blessed me with the icon of St Mitrofan and said as he did it, "From this day you will be my *tolmach* (interpreter) in the work of translating the words of

God." From that time I served as a translator for Father Macarios for about five years, and together we translated prayers and also some of the Gospel.

One night, while we were working on the translation of the Gospels, Father Macarios covered his eyes and sat down with his elbows on the table. I thought he had fallen asleep. He sat motionless like this for over an hour; then he opened his eyes and, pointing to the mouth of the little river Ulala where it flows into the Maima, said, "Is there a spring or stream there?" I replied, "On the other side of the Maima there is a small stream that never freezes up." He said, "An *izbushka* (small house) should be built there." About a week later, he was sitting in the same way and when he opened his eyes, pointing in the same direction, he asked, "Is there a spring there?" I answered, "There is a small river that never freezes there." Father Macarios said, "An *izbushka* should be built there." I was very surprised at his questions because this was in the winter.

Winter, spring, and the Feast of the Trinity passed, and I went to Father Macarios. He said to me jokingly, "When they celebrate, rich people drink wine, but as for us poor people, we drink tea." Then he added, "If you drink tea instead of wine, you will be the healthier for it." After this, we drank tea together, and when we finished, Father Macarios said, "Let's go into the fields for a walk."

We went out and walked along the bank of the Maima opposite the island. At this point, on the bank opposite the island there was a cherry tree. Father Macarios, having stopped beneath the cherry tree, tore off a branch and studied it for a long time, turning it over to see both sides. I thought to myself, "This Father Macarios is like a child who has never seen things before; he studies the branch from the tree and gazes at it in wonder as if he is seeing it for the first time." While I was thinking this, Father Macarios said, "There are veins and little seeds in this branch that the tree itself needs; besides that, there is an inner structure that human eyes cannot see. All this is necessary for the growth of the tree, and God our Creator ordered it to be so." After this, he talked and instructed me for a long time.

Then we came to the mouth of the Ulala, where it flows into the Maima. Raising himself as tall as possible, he looked there very intently and asked, "Isn't there a spring there?" I answered, "There is." We had stopped at the Ulala island, and the water was low. I wanted to make a wooden crossing place, but Father Macarios stopped me and said, "Never mind." Then he said, "They should put a little house by the spring." He gave me a blue five-ruble note and observed, "You will need this." We then went home and, giving me his blessing, he added, "Come and drink tea again with me tomorrow."

The following morning I went to his house, and after we had drunk tea, we went again to the same place. Father Macarios stopped at the same spot as before and again raised himself as tall as he could and, observing the place carefully, said, "Isn't there a spring there?" I answered, "On that side of the Maima on the slope of the hill there is a spring that never freezes over." He said, "They should build a small *izbushka* there." As he said this, he gave me a red ten-ruble note and announced, "You will need this." Then we returned home. When we reached his door, he blessed me and told me to go home. When I got home, I wondered about what had happened. From that time until now, it remains fixed in my memory: Why did he keep asking about the same thing several times? It was a long time before I knew the answer to that question.

[At this point, the author recounts stories about Father Macarios's dealings with other people in the community. —Ed.] One day Father Macarios returned home after serving the Liturgy. A man who had come from Maima went up to him. Father Macarios said to him angrily, "Why did you, impure as you are, come to church today on a feast day? Are there no other days for you to choose?" The man stood there speechless and then said, "I am guilty, Father." Father Macarios said, "Cleanse yourself of your sins and do not do this again."

On another occasion, during Lent, there were a lot of people in the church for confession and prayers in preparation for their communion; some people came from Epikhalka. Among their number was an old man named Andrei Tabakaev. This old man, after his preparation for receiving Holy Communion, was standing in the church when he saw a cockroach crawling along the floor. He went over to it and killed it. Father Macarios saw this, became angry with the old man, and exclaimed, "This was one of God's creations. It was going about its own business whilst you, an intelligent human being, for no good reason of your own, did such a bad thing. You must repent and do contrition for a week before you may approach the holy mystery."

And one evening, having taken tea, Father Macarios said to Mikhail Petrovich, "You, with your love of money, are beginning to resemble Judas, but Stepan Vasilievich (Landyshev, later an archpriest and mission leader) will be a missionary." I heard such a comment from Father Macarios about Mikhail Petrovich Negritsky twice. He was the son of a priest. When he returned home to his father, he married and became a deacon. After this, having been judged by the authorities, he was defrocked and took up a trade. Soon after, I heard that he had died.

Father Macarios always took his evening tea with all those who happened to be in his flat at the time. He drank his tea walking about the room. As he wandered back and forth, he would explain his teaching to all who were present and we, all sitting down, listened to him with great attention that did not wander. Once Father Macarios, as was his habit, was giving us an exposition of part of the holy Scriptures. When Mikhail Petrovich looked toward the door, Father Macarios stopped speaking, walked over to the opposite corner, and stood there without moving. He stood in this way silently for some time. Then, coming over to us again, he asked Mikhail Petrovich, "What did you see by the door?" Mikhail Petrovich answered, "I was watching how a mouse ran across there." Father Macarios said, "The Lord commanded you to study His law, that you should think about it day and night, but perhaps you do not want to study it in this way? Look at that mouse and learn from her. She, in fulfillment of God's laws, is seeking out food whilst you perhaps do not wish to enlarge your soul with good works?" After this, Father Macarios told him to pray to God for His help, and the rest of us he sent off to our own affairs.

Once, Pavel Surochakov, standing at the back of the church behind everyone else, began to laugh. Father Macarios was at the altar. Coming out from there, he called to Pavel from the door and said to him, "People come to church to weep or joyfully to praise and glorify God, but you have come to have a laugh. Do not leave this place until you have wept." He made him go down on his knees and bow many times right to the end of the service.

On another occasion the people of the Ulala district went off to Epikhalka for the St Nicholas Day Feast. There they drank wine and beer. Some of them came back after two days and some after three. When they had returned and on Sunday attended the evening service—served at that time by Father Anastasios—Father Macarios, seeing that the same people had come to church, began to praise them for it and said, "I rejoice that you went to the Feast of St Nicholas, that you traveled there to honor him. You used your horses for this and put up with the cold. St Nicholas will pray for you." Then he asked them, "Did you pray to St Nicholas there? Was there a priest?" "No," they replied. Father Macarios asked, "Perhaps there is a chapel there in honor of St Nicholas?" "No," they replied again. Father Macarios went into the altar and then emerged and said, "Before, I rejoiced, but now I could cry tears of shame. Woe is me! Before, I rejoiced, thinking that you had gone to honor St Nicholas, but in fact you went to anger him. You drank yourselves drunk on wine, you drank beer, you made yourselves sick and vomited, you swore, and you passed out to the great joy of the demons around you. You went to insult the honorable Feast of St Nicholas." After this he made them all bow down to the ground, and they prayed in this way to the end of the service.

Whenever Father Macarios was in Maima, he taught reading and writing to a peasant boy who was brought over from the village of Kokshi. At plowing time, his father, Aleksei Zamyatin, came for him and took him away, and in the winter his father brought the boy back again. Father Macarios said to this Aleksei, "Why did you sprinkle this boy with water?" I was present at the time this conversation took place, and Zamyatin answered, "When he was ill an old woman sprinkled him with a little water." Father Macarios inquired, "Did he get better when he was sprinkled with the water?" Zamyatin replied, "When he was sprinkled, things improved and he got better."

Then Father Macarios declared, "You have angered God and shamed your child. Why did you allow your son to be sprinkled with this satanic water?" And Zamyatin responded, "The old woman blessed the water first and then sprinkled it." But Father Macarios asked, "And what priest blessed it?" Aleksei explained, "The old woman read some prayers over it and then breathed over it." Father Macarios said, "Do you believe in this old woman? Did she call up a demon over the water?" "If this had been from a demon, then the boy would not have gotten better, but when she sprinkled him with the water he improved," Aleksei answered. Then Father Macarios insisted, "There are demons who adopt a benevolent pose. This sort of demon catches a lot of people in his net and makes them his slaves. When one of his comrades causes a man to fall ill, such a false benevolent demon says to his comrade, 'Release this man from his illness and leave him alone; later, we can deceive them all, and they will always call upon us for help. They will not believe in God but will become close to us.' That is how such demons work. Those who are deceived by them will be with them in Hell. Why did you bring shame upon your son with such demonic horror?" Then Father Macarios made him bow low to the ground.

When the inhabitants of Ulala began to seek baptism, one old man—Boris Kochaev—remained unbaptized. Father Macarios tried hard for a long time to persuade him. Every week Father Macarios went to his house and told him about God, and Boris started to regard Father Macarios with hatred. Once, when Boris was sitting in front of his doorway, Father Macarios came to him, sat down near him, and began as usual to talk to him about God, but Boris, out of hatred for him, spoke against him. Father Macarios sat there for a long time talking with him. Having been unable to convince him, Father Macarios said, "I wish you well so that God's blessing may come upon your head. I have discussed this a long time with you, but it seems you do not want God's blessing. From now on it is not me but you who are guilty. God commanded me to talk with you, and I have told you a great deal about God and His truth and goodness; I have told you everything I can. You are saying that your ears do not accept such words; now instead of happiness from God, you will receive unhappiness; instead of God's mercy, God's anger will fall upon your head." Having said this, Father Macarios stroked Boris's head and left. From that time Father Macarios never went to Boris's house. After a month, four hundred rubles fell and were lost from Boris's savings box. In two days all his cattle died— and he had 110 of them. From all his horses, he only had a two-year-old roan foal left. Within two years this Boris, who was formerly rich, became poor. To avoid baptism he moved to Bachat. Once he had lost all the rest of the things he owned, he moved to Mogoite (the second settlement of the Telyeut people who had been baptized). As he had no cattle left, he again moved to Ulala. There he was finally baptized. This Boris lived to be 137 years old and died a Christian. He was given the name Vasilii.

One evening when Father Macarios was at home drinking tea with his disciples, he sang to us. At that time I no longer needed to learn to read and write, so I listened to their singing with pleasure. When they had finished singing, Father Macarios asked me, "Is your son Grigorii well?" "Very well," I answered. "Why is your son is so handsome?" I was silent. He went over to the opposite corner of the room, turned back, and said, "If you have more children, will you dedicate them to the service of God?" I replied, "If I have two, I will give one of them." Father Macarios said, "You should say, 'if it pleases God, I will give them all.'" Then he asked his disciple Stepan Vasilievich, "Did you hear that? He says that if he has two children he will give one of them to the service of God." He gave me his blessing.

When I got home, I found my son was ill, and the next day he was taken by the Lord. After he died, I went to Father Macarios, and just as I went in through the door, he asked, "Is Grigorii Mikhailovich well?" I replied, "He is now with God." Father Macarios crossed himself and said, "Glory be to God!" and to me he added, "Do not be sad; your son will pray to God for you, and later you will be glad. God has more gifts to give you than you have received so far."

A NEW HOME

On another occasion, I came to Father Macarios, who was drinking tea with the psalm singers Anastasios and Father Vasilii. Giving me some tea, he said, "Well, interpreter with the gentle eyes, drink some tea." I began to drink. "Don't cut your hair," he told me. From that moment I let my hair grow. My father noticed this and asked, "Why don't you get your hair cut?" I answered, "Father Macarios told me not to." He said, "It doesn't look good; the Shortsy [inhabitants of another part of the Altai—Ed.] grow it like that." So I started to cut my hair again, but when I went to Father Macarios, he said, "It seems you have stolen some of your own hair!"

On yet another occasion, I came to Father Macarios in the evening. He was teaching us the commandments from God's word. When I started to leave with the others, he said to me, "I want to ask your father about you: Would you like to become one of my people?" I said, "I would if my father will give his blessing." After this he asked my father to come one evening to see him and kept him for a long time. My father, when he came back, said, "He says that he wants me to give him my son as he has been one of his disciples for a long time. I said to him that if he wishes he can take Andrian, but Father Macarios insisted on you. If I give you to him, will you go?" I answered, "He wants to take me to Russia." My father said, "Let Andrian go. He has neither wife nor children."

Soon, while I continued serving as an interpreter for Father Macarios, my father began to get very angry with me, chiding, "You are always going to Father Macarios, and because of this your work is poor." Later, after Andrian's adopted father, Nikolai, died, Andrian returned to my father, his natural father, and came to live with us. My father, placing all his hopes in my younger brother, started to distance himself from me.

It happened in this way: One day, I was getting ready to chop some wood. I put two coats on, but my father said to me, "Where are you thinking of going?" I answered, "Into the forest to cut some wood." My father said, "If you want to cut up some wood then just do it for yourself." I replied, "How do you mean, just for myself—shouldn't I do it for everybody?" My father said, "Well, I am telling you to cut it for yourself only; do you think I am asking you to cut it for other people? You have the *abyz* on your mind all the time; you are always going to him, and you do not do your own work very well. Now leave me and live by yourself." I said, "I don't have a house or food. Where shall I go?" But Father answered, "You are a young man. You can find your own food and build yourself a house. And if you can't do it yourself, then your *abyz* will do it."

I could find nothing to say but sat down and wept. Father asked, "Why are you weeping? Go today and find a place for yourself." I said, "If you do not give me any-thing, how shall I live?" My father replied, "I married you off, and I paid the price for your wife. What should I give you? Go off in the clothes you are wearing." I answered, "Give me at least a cup and a spoon." Father declared, "I will give you nothing." And handing me my fur coat, he said, "You won't get anything apart from this." Taking the coat in my hand and turning to my father, I said, "This coat will not be food and a house for me; take it back. Instead of that, give me your blessing." My father burst into tears. He sat for a moment and then got up and blessed me with the icon of Jesus Christ. After receiving my father's blessing, I left and began to live in a barn that I asked a kinsman to let me use.

For four days I wept and my heart burned with grief; I felt very low and did not know what kind of work to do. On the fifth day, Father Macarios called me to him. When I arrived, he asked, "Why is your face so sad? What has happened?" I did not tell him that I was separated from my father and answered, "No, nothing has happened. I don't know what is wrong." Father Macarios looked at me for some time, took the Gospels and put them on the table, and said, "We will now do some translation from this book." I went up to him and sat down. Father Macarios read to me from the book, and I translated the words into the Altai language. After busying ourselves for some time with the translation, Father Macarios again turned to me and asked, "What stupid thing have you done? Don't try and hide it from me; I can see it in your face. It seems you have done something." I held my breath and could say nothing; then, bursting into tears, I explained, "My father has chased me away with nothing." Father Macarios stood up and said, "Glory be to God! If your father has given you nothing, then your Heavenly Father will provide. If you have not experienced bitter things, you will not know the sweeter ones; if you have not felt the cold, you will not appreciate warmth; if you weep in the evening, you will rejoice in the morning." Then he asked, "Where are you living now?" "In Alexander Poryakin's barn," I replied.

Father Macarios gave me four poods (130 pounds) of flour. The next day he gave me ten rubles and told me to buy a cup and spoon. With this money, I bought the spoons and cups that I needed from Andrei Shchetinin. On the third day, Father Macarios called me over and gave me an axe and a pot. After this, he bought me a gray filly. About a month passed, and he bought a house, yard, and barn for me from Yermolai Shabalin. From then on, in my free time I began to go Father Macarios and work on the translation of the word of God into the Altai language.

Then one day they called to me from the plowed fields. I went there and found many people sitting around. Father Macarios blessed me and said, "I am now going to Russia and I shan't be coming back; please pray for me, a sinner, to our ever-loving Lord, Jesus Christ. I will not forget you and will always pray for you." He said this with tears in his eyes. As for us, seeing his tears we could not hold back our own tears. When we wept, Father Macarios said, "Do not weep, my brethren, we have our Father, Jesus Christ.

We will not be separated from Him, for if we were parted from Him it would be very bad and terrible. If that happened, there would be such grief that people would weep all the time and no one would be able to calm them; there would be continuous suffering that no one could alleviate. You think that I am leaving you and we will never see each other again, but I think that we shall all see each other again in the Kingdom of Heaven. Pray for each other, for God is Love. He loves each and everyone, so you must love each other as you love yourself. I hope to dwell with you in Heaven." As he was saying this, tears welled up in his eyes. Seeing his tears we could not control ourselves but wept also. Father Macarios told us, "Now your spiritual father will be Father Stepan. I am leaving him to replace me and give you all my blessing. May he teach you in the name of God all the good things you must know. As you listened to me, so listen to him." In this way Father Macarios taught us good ways right up until his departure for Russia, like a dying father leaves his guidance to his children. He left. We, left behind, wept like orphans who had lost their father. [Father Macarios had to leave Altai in 1843 for reasons of health.—Ed.]

CHAPTER 2

Interpreter of Faith

When Father Macarios left for Russia, I began to work very hard with the plow. After I plowed all the level places, I had great difficulties plowing the sloping land. When someone has a lot of horses, this is easy, for he can harness them to the plow, but it was hard for me as I had few horses.

One night around this time, I could not get to sleep. I was thinking about working out some way of plowing the slopes and how to make a wooden plow for this. Then I suddenly thought in my mind of a way as clearly as if I saw it before my very eyes. I quickly made such a wooden plow, tried it out, and found plowing was easy even with only two horses. The clumps of earth that were lifted by such a plow turned easily on the slopes of the hill. This plow moved freely in one furrow. I was very pleased and thanked God.

After this I set about learning many different skills. I set up a mill, and it worked very well. I was glad and thanked God again. I learned also how to forge iron and how to work with leather. I learned carpentry and how to saw boards. I even learned how to do vaccinations. All these trades were useful to me, but they did not make me rich because my mind was on other things.

Once Father Stepan called me to him and said, "We will translate the word of God. Be my interpreter, and I will pay you forty rubles a year." I answered, "I have a wife and children. Forty rubles will be a very small sum for me." Father Stepan insisted, "You try it for a year and then I will increase the sum." So I served as his interpreter for four years. But in the four years the sum was increased by only ten rubles.

During this four-year period when I served as a translator, we worked on the translation of the word of God into the Telyeut language. Whenever people came to be baptized, with Father Stepan's blessing I taught them the prayers in the Altai language and explained the holy faith to them. Sometimes Father Stepan himself spoke to them in Russian and I translated.

Two years after I became Father Stepan's translator, a certain civil servant called Nikolai Ivanovich Ananin came from Kuznetsk. He stayed with Father Stepan and sent for me. "I am concerned with gathering information about the ways of life of native peoples who speak your language—their songs, their proverbs, their traditions and habits. I have a lot of such material about the peoples of the Kuznetsk region, but I have not found a person who is competent to translate it. I have heard that you can do such translations, so I have sent for you to work with me on them." I answered, "I serve Father Stepan as an interpreter and cannot give you a decision on this myself. Ask Father Stepan." And he replied, "I have asked him on your behalf, and he says he is willing to release you to work with me while I'm here." At that moment Father Stepan came through the door from another room and said to me, "I am going to Biysk, so you can go and work as an interpreter him." And for more than a week I translated our legends into Russian with this Ananin. When Father Stepan returned, Ananin said, "You can continue to write out for me the beliefs of the native peoples here, their songs, their stories, and the traditions that have come down to them from past times." Then he gave me two rubles and left. I gave everything that I wrote about these things to Father Stepan, who sent them to Nikolai Ivanovich by post. Ananin came again the next year and took me with him to the town of Biysk. I stayed there nine days, busy with translation. For this he gave me three rubles and left. Three months later Father Stepan received a document that said that I should go to Kuznetsk, and in five days I arrived at Ananin's place. I spent about two months there. When I had finished the translation work, Nikolai Ivanovich gave me ten rubles and I returned home.

I have not seen him since then, but he said to me, "I will send you some more money." However, I never received anything else from him.

When I returned from Kuznetsk, it was already spring. The water levels in Ulala were very high then. There was a festival around that time, and many young people gathered at my place, where I taught them to sing church music. Suddenly, my house began to shake! Some people laughed and said, "There's a lot of people here. The house can't hold them all and it's trembling." However, others said, "Perhaps the water is getting near!" And Ilya Korolkov offered, "I'll go and see." Indeed, the water of the Ulala River had reached the top of its banks. Just as Ilya Korolkov opened the door, the house leaned to one side. Quickly, some people ran out through the door while others jumped through the windows, and such things as were in the house were pulled out through the windows. They got only one box out through the door. As there were a lot of people, they managed to stop the water from carrying away the logs from the house by pulling them up onto the bank. Nevertheless, as some of the timber was washed away and much of it ruined by mud, it was not possible to rebuild the *izba* (small house). So on that day we sang in the morning and wept in the evening. I had no *izba*. The next day I went to Father Stepan, who, on account against my wages, bought for me an unfinished *izba* from Mikhail Naurchakov. In the summer I moved it and erected it.

One day Father Stepan sent me with a missionary, Father Arsenii, to the Telyeut-Shorts people in Kuznetsk. After spending the night on the road, we arrived in the village of Yeniseisk the next day. When I was sitting in the coachman's house, a man came in, kissed my hand, and said, "Greetings, angel from God!" He said this many times and each time kissed my hand. I asked, "Where do you live?" He answered, "I have come a long way." "What is your name?" He said, "So you don't know me. I saw you in the church in the village of Bachat." When he said this, I recognized him. It was the man my uncle and I met when we went to the Feast of St Nicholas. My uncle Chenosh had said, "This is Yevsei, the fool for Christ." Recognizing him, I asked, "Aren't you Yevsei?" He said something to me, but I did not understand him, and then he went away again quickly. I was surprised at this, and since that time I have never forgotten him.

Father Arsenii and I set off from that place and in three days came to Kuznetsk. We spent one day there and then went on to the settlements of the Shorts people upriver. These Shorts people live in the Russian manner: Their *izby* and clothes are in the Russian style; only their women dress differently. In their houses they have icons, but in some of them there are also small idols decorated with stones. When I saw this I asked, "You have been baptized, haven't you? Why do you have these pagan idols, then?" They answered, "Although we have been baptized, how can we live without these charms?"

I asked, "Do you pray to God in the Russian way?" "Of course we pray!" they said. Then I inquired, "What do you call God?" and the people responded, "Father Nicholas, or Elijah, the prophet." But some of them said, "Jesus Christ is also God." So I explained, "Only Jesus Christ is God. There is no other God but Him, and St Nicholas and the prophet Elijah are not gods: They were pleasing to God so now they dwell in a beautiful and joyful place." Some of the people said, "We have heard that Jesus Christ is the true God, but we do not pray to Him very much." I spoke to them for a short time about the true God. I also asked them, "Are all the people in this place baptized?" "Yes, we have all been baptized," they answered. "And do the priests teach you to pray to God?" They replied, "Sometimes they do teach us," and I asked, "What do the priests teach you?" "They teach us to pray to God." I exclaimed aloud, "Only that?" But they countered, "How can they teach us! We do not fully understand the Russian language, and our wives and children don't know it at all."

We spent one day in this village. The next day, we continued up the Mras River and were met by a man who was transporting a load of birch bark piled on a wooden frame. Father Arsenii's horse took fright, stomped the ground, and ran wild. We could not catch up with it and hold it. When the horse reared up, Father Arsenii fell. His foot was caught in the stirrup, and for some time he was dragged along the ground. Finally, he managed to free himself. When we went up to him to lift him up, he said, "Wait a moment, don't touch me; I'll lie still for a bit." I asked, "How are things then? Is everything all right?" He answered, "All is well." We caught his horse, lifted him up into his saddle, and went on.

We arrived at a settlement called Mys. I asked the Shorts people there, "It seems you have been baptized? Do you know God?" "We know Him," they answered. "What is God called?" "Jesus Christ," said some, but others said, "Mikola." So I explained to them the difference between God and St Nicholas.

Then we came to a settlement higher up the river Mras whose name I have forgotten. A dense, dark forest grew on both sides of the road in this place. The carrier who drove the factory carts lived there, and we stayed with him. While we were there, two men came in. I asked them, "It seems you have no plowland here. How do you feed yourselves?" They answered, "In the spring we catch fish and ship them in boats to Kuznetsk. We sell them there, and with the money we make we buy bread and return with the boats carried on poles. Also some of us sell honey and buy bread. And the wealthier people do some trading." After talking with me, they went home.

Father Arsenii suggested to me, "I would like you to go round the houses here, and if you meet any who have not been baptized, speak to them about it as much as you can." I visited six houses. In some of them I saw icons and in others pagan charms. I asked the people, "How does it come about that in some houses there are icons and in others charms?" They answered, "Look, we are not Russians who do not have idols, but when there is a fever, how can we live without charms?" So I spoke with them about the Ten Commandments and about our holy faith.

When I left them and was going down the street, I met two men who were planing boards. Two others were sitting by them, and I sat with them. The first two came up to me, sat down, and asked, "Where do you come from?" I told them where and by what river I lived, where we were going, and the reason for our journey. While we were talking in this way, about twenty people who were going down the road gathered around us. I asked them, "Have you all been baptized?" And they answered, "Here everyone has been baptized." I questioned further, "Do you know the name of God?" "We know." "Who do you speak to when you pray?" They replied, "We pray to Father Mikola and also the prophet Elijah." I said, "And do you pray to Jesus Christ?" They answered, "We have heard of Jesus Christ, but we don't know much about Him." I wondered aloud, "But doesn't the priest teach you?" They explained to me, "The priest comes here, gathers a group together, and soon returns home." Again I asked, "And so the priest doesn't teach you?" They answered, "How can we be taught when we don't know Russian?"

Then I tried to explain everything to them, beginning with Adam right up to the birth of Christ, and also about the resurrection of the dead, the second coming of Christ, and the judgment of the living and dead. They said, "In the old days, at the time of our ancestors, some priest came here with some soldiers and baptized them and then went home. We, their descendants, have been baptized but are ignorant. We veer from one idea to another. We do not have anyone who could teach us the word of God. Who could guide us? It is for this reason that we still keep idols in our houses." I warned them, "You should not believe what the shaman tells you. The shamans do not know the true God; deceived by the devil, they cast spells over you." They villagers replied, "From ancient times we have honored the land on which we live, the water, and the sky with sacrifices; how can we dare to stop honoring them now?" So I told them about God, how with a word He healed the sick and raised the dead. Then I got up and set out toward my lodging.

As I walked along the street, I saw about thirty men who were fishing as they sailed down the Mras in boats. Having spotted them, I stopped and waited at the place where they would have to drag in their nets. When they were pulling in the nets, I noticed that they were fishing with three sweep nets. In the one that was pulled out first, there were eight taimen, in the next, perch and pike, and in the third, *chebaki*. Besides these, I did not see any other fish.

After I got back to my lodging, I set out with Father Arsenii by boat down the Mras. We arrived at a village that was upriver from Kuznetsk, where our carriage was waiting. From there we went to Kuznetsk. We spent the night, and the next day we went to the Baiatsky Telyeut people.

There, among the Telyeut people, we met some who were born of baptized parents, but their parents had brought them up unbaptized and married their sons and daughters to unbaptized people. We would not have known of them, but Alexander, who was newly baptized by Father Stepan, lived in the Ulu settlement. This Alexander made a list for us of all who were born of baptized parents but had remained until old age unbaptized. We asked him, "Why were they not baptized when their parents had been baptized?" Alexander explained, "In former times, a priest came here to baptize the children of those who had received baptism, but their parents did not bring them in to receive this rite. This was because although the parents had been baptized, they had not heard the teachings of our holy faith and, living among unbaptized people, they did not know their own faith and did not arrange for their children to be baptized. These ancestors are dead; the children who are here now are their grandchildren and they remained unbaptized."

Then we gathered the people of Ulu together and asked them about this, and they replied, "How can we know whether we were born of baptized or unbaptized parents; we ourselves don't know." But some of them said, "True, we did hear about this from our parents." So

I spoke with them about God and the holy divine faith. On our third day in Ulu, we baptized thirty people. One would not receive baptism because he respected the shamans. We spent three more days there and taught them about the faith.

Father Arsenii and I returned home (from the Baiatsky Telyeuts), and I worked some more as an interpreter. But the small wages that I received proved insufficient for food and clothing for four children, so I ceased to be an interpreter and took up trade. Thanks be to God, I was able to support myself in this way, and in my free time I translated the holy Scriptures into the Altai language and read them to those who did not know Russian. Those who loved the word of God came and listened.

ON MISSIONARY ROADS

After this, I planned another trip. I wanted to take two people and my wife and brother-in-law fishing in Lake Telets. When we reached a little river called the Isha, we saw that a civil servant called Sosunov had brought a group of people together to sort out a legal case, and two or three of them were encamped under the trees. When I came up to them, one of the Altai people, called Suuluk, said to me, "Glory be to God that you have come! These Tubints people are helping a thief who is one of their own. It seems they have made friends with the administrator and are sorting out my affair among themselves. There is no one to speak up for my side; help me, for

God's sake! Their interpreter doesn't know our language very well."

I explained his grievance to the administrator, and he gave orders that Suuluk should have satisfaction. The Tubints people wanted to beat me up and asked, "Why are you putting your nose into our business?" But when the state interpreter, Karbyshev, arrived, they stopped threatening me.

The Tubints people are like a flock without a shepherd: anyone who is wealthy is accounted a leader, and anyone who is poor is like a scared fish and fears any sort of judgment. Among them, the poor never make any complaints about grievances. When I asked, "Why don't you go to court over your grievances?" they replied, "How can he who does not have big herds of cattle and bags of money go to court! We are as frightened as hares and silent as fish. We are ordinary people who know nothing of law. What could we know? Our leaders like to hear only from those who have black sable and fat animals...."

My small group spent the night there, and the next day we set out toward the baptized native people who lived in the settlement of Ynyrga. Although I wanted to enter the houses of the newly baptized, I found them empty because they were not using the *izby* built for them by the missionaries but preferred to erect for themselves birchwood yurts, where they live, sitting around the fire laid out in the middle. I asked them, "Why don't you live in the houses instead of sitting in the middle of so much smoke and straining your eyes?" They replied, "We do not know how to live in Russian *izby*, and we do not know how to arrange our lives in them in the Russian way; for us these birchwood yurts, where we can smoke and prepare our oatmeal, are better."

I inquired, "Do you plow the fields like the Russians?" The people answered, "We sow corn, working the soft soil with *abyls* (hoes), and we do some work for the Russians so that with them we can sow some wheat." Then I asked, "Why don't you make plows and do some plowing?" They explained, "We don't know how to because we have not been taught to do that." And I exclaimed, "You're too lazy to learn! If you plowed the land like the Russians, then you wouldn't get into debt for food." They replied, "It would be good if we could make Russian plows and plow the land. It is true, too, that we are lazy." I wondered aloud, "You don't sow much wheat, and you won't work in the Russian way, so how are you going to find the means to pay the tsar and buy food for yourselves?" The people told me, "When the summer comes, we will prepare the hay for the cattle; when it is harvest time for the nuts, we will gather nuts; when the autumn comes, we will take up work with the animals." I asked, "Do you make much from gathering nuts and working with the animals?" They answered, "From a good year's nut harvesting we make enough for our bread, but when the nuts do not grow well, then from animal work alone there is not much left to pay the taxes. Those who do not have enough to pay their taxes to the state hire themselves out to the Russians for a year's work."

I will describe now how things are with the people of Ynyrga in the place where they live. Around them are dark forests, covering the whole expanse from the snowy peaks of the mountains. The river Ynyrga flows from the west into the Karakoksha; the source of this Ynyrga is in a high mountain called Kara Kaya (Dark Cliff). The Tubints people who live near this mountain offer sacrifices to it. The Tubints told me, "In the old days, when the Mongol warriors came, the god who saved our ancestors from them was this very mountain with the cliff, and every summer we offer a sacrifice to it. And now, with the nuts growing on it and other things we extract from it, it gives us our bread and pays our taxes." I asked them, "How did this hill you call Dark Cliff save your ancestors from the Mongol invaders?" They answered, "When the Mongols were following our people, our ancestors offered a sacrifice as they climbed the hill. The hill then became impassible, like night in the dark, black forest. Then the Mongols couldn't find their way and turned back home."

The high source of the Karakoksha is in the snow-covered mountains to the south, and it flows into the Biya four *versts* (three miles) below Kebezeni. The river Uimen flows from the eastern mountains and the Sara-Koksha flows from the western mountains into the Kara-koksha above the Ynyrga. The river Pryzha flows from the western mountains into the Biya above Kebezeni. All these rivers flow from the snow-covered mountains that lie between the Biya and the Katunya. All are full of fish, and from their sources in the mountains to their mouths they are lined with gray rocks along the banks and dark forests. Cedars, firs, birch, aspen, and yellow and white poplars grow along the banks. Pine, cherry trees, rowan trees, snowball trees, raspberries, black and red currants, acacias, elderberries, dogberries, black poplars, spruce, bulrushes, blackthorn, hawthorn, and honeysuckle grow at the mouths of the rivers.

Now I will tell you something about the animals. Most of all you can find squirrels, ermine, marmots, beavers, water rats, three kinds of mice, polecats, foxes, hares, wild goats, lynx, bears, white deer, elk, and sable. I will tell you of the fish too: pike, *kuskuch, burbot, harius, balbakbash, uriup*, and *tilmai.*

My group of travelers spent three days at Ynyrga and then went down to the mouth of the Kokshi and spent the night there. The following day we crossed the Biya River and arrived at Kebezeni, where we spent the night. There were three Russian settlements and two houses belonging to some newly baptized people. The Tirgesh Kergesh clan traveled along the small rivers that came down from the mountains, to the east of Kebezeni. These Tirgesh natives are an honorable people; they do not get involved in any kind of thieving. We stayed in Kebezeni until the spring. After the Feast of Pascha, I set out to find wild bees and found nine nests. These nine nests gave eleven swarms. In all in that year, I found twenty nests.

We stayed in the area until St Elijah's day, and then we traveled on to Lake Telets to do some fishing. There for about a month we caught herrings: in all we caught forty poods (1,200 pounds). The Tirgesh people from that district fish at night. The shallows where they fished are no more than ten *sazhens* (25 yards) long, and from such a short space they caught more fish than we did, although the shallows where we fished were fifty *sazhens* (125 yards) long. This is because they fish in the shallows by having some people drag a line along the bottom, pushing it along with their feet, while others, standing in boats, drag a line along on poles. Doing it this way, they caught more fish than we could: at one time they were able to catch three times the numbers we caught, and their catches were better than ours. Whenever they took a break from their work, they would sit on the bank and smoke their pipes.

While we were there, I heard them sing the following song:

> How beautiful is the Golden Lake
> With its shining white mists!
> How tasty are its fish,
> Which feed its people!
> How beautiful are its mountains,
> Richly covered with dark forest.
> How fertile are its flocks of wild animals,
> With which it feeds its people.

When we had used up all our supplies, my wife and I went on horseback to Kebezeni. We spent two days there, and once we had gathered supplies, we set off back to the lake. On the way we called at the yurt that belonged to Taduzhek on the bank of the lake. An old man with a gray, shaking head was sitting in the yurt. "Grandad, how old are you?" I asked. The old man said, "Ninety-seven years old." So I asked, "How much longer will you live?" And the old man replied, "My son! Do I have much longer to live? Maybe I will die today, and if not today, then tomorrow. Can't you see me properly? I am sitting at the very edge of the burial pit. I am awaiting death each day." I said, "You are awaiting death, but where will you live after death? Tell me, most respected old man." The old man responded, "How can I know, my son? We grew up like the beasts of the field: you should know better than I, for you read God's book and talk to God." I said to him, "Please, let me tell you something from God's book: do you believe?" The old man asked, "What more is there to believe than God's words?" And I explained, "There is one God, Jesus Christ, who created Heaven and earth, the birds that fly, the animals that run, and all that breathes and all people. There is no God but Him, and whoever does not believe in Him cannot enter His shining light, which is full of His blessing, for God is the greatest light and the greatest good. His light is never dimmed, and the grace of God never weakens but exists forever, always and eternal. Those people who do not believe in Him cannot live in His blessed light."

Then the old man said, "We too believe in God and also in Aza (the demon)." I questioned him, "What god do you believe in? Tell me his name." "We worship and offer sacrifices to Altai-khan, the khan of the heavens, and also bring offerings of food to the high mountains and rivers that feed us like mothers." I asked, "Who is the greatest of these?" "The greatest of all—the father of all—is Rich Ulgen" (the good divinity), the old man answered, "and after him Erlik" (evil god of the underworld). I wondered, "And your soul—which of these will have it?" He said, "We will go to the father of all, the father of Erlik." "And nothing will be left for the others?" I asked. The old man smiled and said, "All these people are descended from our forefather Erlik; of course, they will go back to him, for all people come from him; we are his descendants and wherever he is we will be too."

I explained to him, "Erlik is not God and Ulgen is not God; the one God who created all that is visible and invisible is Jesus Christ, and all the rest are not gods. You worship mountains and water. They are not gods but creations of the true God. Therefore, instead of worshipping created things, you should worship our Lord, Jesus Christ, who created these mountains and waters, and you should give Him thanks for them." The old man asked, "How should I pray to Him? Explain it to me." I answered, "'My God, Jesus Christ, You created all the rivers, all the mountains. You created the heavens and earth and all that is in them. Thanks be to Thee!' That is how you should pray." The old man was silent, so I continued, "If someone built a house for a man, full of all comforts, who would that man thank for it? Would he give thanks to the house or to the person who built the house?" The old man answered, "Of course, he would not give thanks to the house but to him who gave it." I said, "Why then do you give thanks to the sky and earth and all that is in them and not to God who created them all?"

The old man answered, "And what has water got to do with this? Tell me, my son." I answered, "For the sake of the sins of all people, the true God, Jesus Christ, came down from Heaven to earth in the womb of the Holy Virgin and took upon Himself the body of a man. He was crucified on a cross, died, and on the third day rose again from the dead. Then, having remained on earth for forty days, He rose to Heaven. Therefore, when a person, in remembrance of the three-day death and burial, is immersed three times in water in the name of God, he is born again from the water and the Holy Spirit. In this way the newly born soul of that person shines with God's light and takes on the likeness of God. The baptized person is clothed in Christ; therefore, he becomes like the Son of God."

The old man said, "For what sins do the unbaptized not enter God's light?" Then I explained everything to him, beginning with Adam and the fall, about the birth of Christ, about how He suffered, how He rose again on the third day and on the fortieth day ascended into Heaven, and how He will again come to earth on the last day to judge the living and the dead. After listening to this with great attention, the old man said, "Today or tomorrow I will die, my son. Without a priest here, who will baptize me?" I answered, "I will send a man with a note to the priest, and meanwhile you stay here and learn some prayers." The old man appealed to me, "Give me your cross, which will be God's sign for me." I placed my cross upon him and taught him a little how to pray to God.

My wife and I set out from that place and returned to the lake. When I was fishing there, Father Stepan sent a man to tell me to go to Kebezeni. When I arrived, Father Stepan said to me, "When I wanted to baptize that old man whom you had prepared for baptism, he said to me, 'I will not be baptized until that man who gave me the cross comes here.' This is why I sent for you." Then I asked the old man, "Why won't you accept baptism from this priest?" The old man answered, "I have never seen this priest before and refused baptism, thinking that perhaps some false priest wants to baptize me." I assured him, "This is our elder priest from Ulala, Father Stepan." He said, "Well, then, go ahead and baptize me." And Father Stepan baptized him and gave him the name Peter.

The next day Father Stepan and I went to our place by the lake. The day we arrived, my workers, who were collecting wood nearby, found a tree with bees in it. We got about a pood (thirty-six pounds) of honey from it. The following day Father Stepan gave me several crosses and said, "I am giving you my blessing and these crosses so that you can give them to the people who seek baptism." Then Father Stepan went back to Ulala.

BAPTISM OF TIBAN

One day a while later, I was sitting in my camp drinking tea, and two men approached. "Greetings!" they said. "Greetings!" I replied. "What's the news?" "Nothing special." "Are you catching many fish?" "It's not bad; we catch some. Where are you going, brothers?" They replied, "Only as far as here. We are hungry. Is there any bread?" I answered, "There is. Wait a little and I'll cook you some fish; it is good to eat it with bread." I cooked them some fish and gave it to them, and they began to converse with me more intimately. I asked, "Where are you going?" "From here we are going to Cholyshman," they answered. "Why do you need to be in Cholyshman? Why are you in such a hurry to get there, without bothering to gather any nuts?" I asked. They just said, "We need to be there." I tried again: "What's the urgency?" One of them answered, "Last winter my father died, and my friend's wife also died. This is the reason we are traveling to Cholyshman. A shaman, Nias, lives there; we want to bring him back with us so that he can purify our yurts of their uncleanness." I asked, "How come your yurts are unclean?" And they answered, "Among our people there is the belief that when somebody dies, the yurt in which this happened is unclean from the presence of *aldachi*, or the 'angel of death,' and this presence, they say, may take away other souls if it is not chased away by a powerful shaman. Otherwise, it may take away all the people nearby." I wondered, "Isn't there among the Tirgesh people a shaman to be found who could chase it away?" They answered, "Among all that clan there is no shaman as strong as the shaman Nias from Cholyshman."

Then I told them, "God in Jesus Christ, who was able to create Heaven and earth, alone can purify a man of all evil and drive demons from him; apart from Him, no human shaman can cleanse a man." They said, "Yes, our shamans, when they drive out demons, also call upon God." I asked, "What god do your shamans call upon?" One of them said, "The father of all, Rich Ulgen, and also they call upon the master of earth and water." I said, "Earth and water, all visible and invisible things, all that is living and all that is upon this earth, were created by the true God in six days, and He created all the children of Adam. Apart from Him, there are no other gods. The one that you believe in, calling him god, is not God. God is not the earth, nor the sky, nor the moon nor sun, and He is not a tall mountain or the waters of the sea or something like that. The true God—Jesus Christ—He always was, is, and always will be."

At this the younger of the men, whose name was Tiban, said, "You must tell me about this Adam whom you called father of all people. Tonight I will bring you some fish." I answered, "If I were too lazy to explain the word of God to someone who simply asks me to do so, then I would commit a great sin, for God said, 'Do not turn away those who come to seek me.' For this reason it would be a sin for me to be too lazy to explain the word of God to those who wish to hear it, but it would also be a sin for he who, having heard the word of God, does not believe it." Tiban answered, "Why should we not believe a person who has studied the holy books?"

After this I explained everything to him, beginning with Adam and up to the birth of Christ and then about the time following this, about the resurrection of the dead and the Last Judgment. It was already beginning to get dark. The young man stayed the night at my camp, and the other one went to spend the night in another yurt. During the night, the young man went fishing with us.

In the morning Tiban said, "In a couple of days I will bring my people here; you can talk with them about God." I answered, "Why not let me talk with them? Bring them along."

And so Tiban did not go on to the shaman at Cholysh-man but went back to his people. His friend, called Chal, who had come with him, went on to Cholyshman and the shaman, Nias. In four days, Tiban returned, bringing with him his mother, sister, and younger brother.

As soon as they arrived, I cooked some fish for them and spoke to them from the holy Scriptures, and they listened to my talk with great pleasure. Evening came upon us, and they spent the night with us. In the morning

Tiban said, "Today we are going to help Orozhok. People might want to beat me up if I want to be baptized; come and see me later." Once he had said this, Tiban set off with his people to help Orozhok.

I took my gun and set out to shoot grouse over their plowed fields, where they grow corn, and met about thirty people who were reaping. Some of them were reaping with a sickle and others pulled the plant up by the root, held it to the ground with a foot, and cut it with a knife. I wondered, "Why do you make such a hard job of it when you could cut it with a sickle?" They answered, "Among us there are some people who have never in their whole lives held a sickle, and for this reason, out of old habit we grab the corn and cut it with a knife." I asked, "Wouldn't it be possible to learn how to use a sickle?" "If the peddlers hadn't sold us some sickles, then we wouldn't have even these few. But because we are used to the old ways, we forget to buy sickles when we are among Russians."

After this conversation, I returned to my camp. The sun was setting beyond the mountain. Two men came to me from Orozhok by boat and said, "The boss would like you to come to see him. Will you come?" My wife and I got into the boat and set off to see Orozhok. When we arrived, we found forty people there, all drunk. A fire was laid in the middle of them, and above it was a three-legged stand with a large cauldron in which they were cooking whole animal bones. Orozhok noticed our arrival, took us by the hand, and sat us down upon a piece of felt where he was sitting. He took a leather flask of wine, put it in front of us, and said, "That is something special I have brought." As was my habit, I took it in my hands and said, "I have taken it, I have drunk of it, pass it on to others." Orozhok called a young lad over to him and said, "Give them some of this!" The young fellow poured wine for us from the flask and gave it to us. I drank some of it with my host, but my wife did not drink.

At that time they served up meat on big wooden platters and began to eat. I watched and saw that none of them washed their hands but devoured the bones while holding them with hands that were still dirty from work. When the fat from the meat mixed with the dirt on their hands and ran down their arms, they licked it up from their palms with their tongues and put their fingers in their mouths and sucked them. They also drank wine. The night became very dark, and some began to sing but others started fighting. Some were pulled by the braiding in their hair, and others fought with their heads. Once they had finished fighting, like children they again forgot all about their anger and they drank and smoked together. But after sitting still for a short time, they again started to make a row. I could see that they wanted to beat up Tiban because he wished to be baptized. Tiban, when he saw me, said, "For the sake of God in Heaven and the tsar on earth, I want to be baptized. They want to beat me for this; please, intervene for me." So I said, "You people must not touch him; if you beat him I shall write a complaint to the court." Orozhok declared, "You say right. And you people leave him alone." After this some of them embraced Tiban and kissed him, but others simply sat still. Then Tiban left. I waited for a while, but as he did not return, my wife and I set out for our camp. When we got home, there was Tiban sitting—waiting.

A half hour after we returned, eight men came after us in a boat. Tiban, meanwhile, lay down and took off his boots. Among the eight was a ceratin Danil. He said to Tiban, "Orozhok wants to see you. Put your boots on quickly and come with us." Tiban asked, "What does Orozhok want with me in the night? I am not coming." They said, "Orozhok wants to make you head of the family in place of your father." Tiban answered, "If Orozhok wants to do that, why does he need to send a whole regiment to get me? You want to set Orozhok against me because I want to be baptized. I am not coming!" Then they started to put his boots on him. Tiban grabbed the boots and threw them away.

During all this we were lying down and watching what would happen. From somewhere they got a rope and began to tie up Tiban. Tiban cried out, "For God's sake, free me from these people." Then I said to my brother-in-law, Yakov, and my workers, "Chase them away with a whip." Yakov and the workers got up, and those people who had come ran away like scared animals. Some got into the boat, and others ran along the bank. Once they had gone, we all went off to sleep.

The next day more people came from Orozhok: eight women and four men. They said to Tiban, "You, Tiban, are a useful and valuable man for our people; we wanted to make you head of the family in place of your father. But it seems you are withdrawing from us; now, if you get yourself baptized, then you will not be one of us, and of course, your heart will be apart from us." Tiban replied, "Do you think I want to die, that I want to go away and change the feelings of my heart toward you? Perhaps you think that after baptism I will forget you and fly away like a bird or run away from you like a wild animal? Why do you weep for me?" Some of the women indeed wept over him; some abused him and some said, "What made you think of getting baptized, brother? Perhaps you were short of bread? Perhaps you were lacking in clothing? Or did your relatives insult you? Why have you become angry and left us, and why do you want to be baptized? If you need something, then don't be shy—tell us! We will help you with all your needs. See, all your relatives are here; aren't you sorry for them? Put aside this idea of yours."

Tiban said, "I have already given it thought: God is above, the tsar below, and I am not returning to you. It would be better for you to go home and not come after me." Then they all burst into tears. When Tiban saw his mother, sisters, and brothers weeping, he could not hold back his own tears. But he said, "Now send a note to the priest; he can come and baptize us."

The next day I placed on four of them the crosses that Father Stepan had given me. Three days later, Miron Kulashev, from the village of Maiminsk, which is not far from Ulala, came to see me. I wrote a letter to Father Stepan and sent it to him by Kulashev. About a month after I sent the letter, Father Vasilii and Father Smaragd came from Ulala and baptized them. Tiban was given the name Ioann; his mother, the name Anna; his sister, Evdokia; and his younger brother, Simeon. Apart from them, five more people were baptized, making a total of nine.

PRAYERS ANSWERED BY ST NICHOLAS

After the baptism, I set out with my wife, two workers, and my brother-in-law to Cholyshman, and on the way we did some fishing and trading. When we had sailed to the end of the lake, five *versts* (three miles) from Artybash, we stopped for the night and did some fishing. When we wanted to draw in our net, it got stuck and would not move at all. We made a fire on the bank and sat and rested awhile, and then we tried to move it again, but without success. In the prow of our boat, there was an iron framework on which we made our fires. We placed our fire upon it, rowed over to the net, and noticed that it was not to be seen in the water. Only the end could be seen. When we pulled the end that we could see, we still could not move it. We lost hope and sat by the fire to get warm. I began to feel despair in my soul and prayed in my heart to St Nicholas. After a short time, I felt a certain unexpected lightness in my soul. I became more cheerful. Everyone was sitting there in despair, but I stood up joyfully and said, "Well, then, lads, get up: St Nicholas will help us, and we will now be able to pull up the net." Three of us pulled, and the net moved easily. We looked the net over, and there was not a single tear. Then one of my workers, called Stepan, called out, "O, Lord, Lord, thanks be to Thee! Father Nicholas, you helped us."

That night we did not try to do any more fishing and I, not able to fall asleep from excitement, said to myself, "You should set up a chapel on this bank of the lake to honor St Nicholas." The next day we sailed along the right bank of the lake in the direction of the river Kamyga and got as far as the mouth of a small river called Yalo-ashu, which flows into Lake Telets. This place has flat banks mostly covered with small birch trees. I asked the local people, "How does it happen that here by the Yalo-ashu these beautiful and dense birch trees are growing?" They said, "Before, Tyurgets people lived here, but they began to die of fever. To save themselves from the sickness, they moved further down Lake Telets to Artuash, where we live on both banks of the Biya. This dense and beautiful forest grew on what was formerly our fathers' plowed fields."

After this we came to the river Kamga and spent the night there. This spot lies on the bank of Lake Telets and faces the rising sun in the spring. On its left bank, it is covered with forest as far as the taiga at the top of the mountains. The tops are covered with snow and gray outcrops of rock. On the right bank is the bare, high taiga, relieved only in places by groups of trees. The people who live nearby say that there are a lot of bears, deer, and other wild animals there, and in and around the Kamga, they say there are many fish and otters and also a large number of sable. They also say that there are a lot of bees in the forest near the rivers.

We spent two days at the mouth of the Kamga and then went on further along the right bank. Toward the end of the lake, we came upon tall rocks projecting out of the water. We sailed in the gap between these rocks. The local people, known as the Toolos, call this Airy-Tash, or the split stone. They say that in olden times the Mongol army, sailing on rafts between these stones, perished in the waters during a storm. On our way we came across a river that tumbled down the rocks—a waterfall. The rock down which it fell was very high. When we went past it and tried to talk among ourselves, it was impossible to hear the sound of a human voice on account of the noise of the water. The sound of the falling water is like a strong wind. We traveled further and saw that another river flowed from the east into the lake; on both sides were high mountains and rocks. This river is called the Kopsha, and on the mountaintops nearby there is snow-covered taiga.

Not far from the mouth of this river, we stopped for the night.

The next day we reached the Toolos people who live near the river Chyulyush. We passed the night there and bought twelve poods of nuts for fifteen kopecks a pood. By the Chyulyush there were twelve yurts. Many tree stumps are in the midst of the lands that these people plow. I asked, "Why don't you plow level and clear ground rather than work among these stumps?" And they answered, "We would plow the clear land, but the soil is bad there; it is difficult to work it with a hoe. In the places where we intend to work the soil, three years in advance we cut down a dense forest of small trees. When this deadwood has been lying there for three years, grass begins to grow under the branches. Besides that, the mice and moles dig the soil and it becomes softer."

I also asked, "Is there a heavy snowfall in these parts?" They told me, "In this place, beginning from the middle of the mountains downward, the snow slips down and so it is not very deep, and the snow that falls near the river is carried away by the wind. This is why we can keep sheep and goats during the winter."

We went further. The mouth of the Cholyshman could be seen flowing into the lake. Intending to reach it quickly in order to spend the night there, we rowed harder, but before we could manage to get there, night came and it became very dark. There were two fires visible at the mouth of the Cholyshman; we wanted to reach them, so we sailed forward in the dark. When we were getting near the place where we could see one of the fires, our boat ran aground and could not reach the bank. We managed to turn back to the deeper part of the lake and searched for the main channel of the Cholyshman, where it flows into the lake. Meanwhile, the waters of the lake became very choppy from the wind, which had grown stronger, and we found it difficult to row past the sandbank and find the correct channel. We were very glad and thanked God when we succeeded.

Rowing a little up the river Cholyshman, we came out on the side of the bank where we had seen the fire. There were no people by the fire, but a lot of wood had been collected for it. The people had run away when they heard our voices. In this place I harpooned two large fish, and we cooked one of them and ate it.

The next day, when we were going up the Cholyshman, using poles to push our boat, we found an island with two latticed yurts. Intending to approach these yurts to do some trading, we ran aground on a small beach near them and made tea. Two people came to us from the yurt: an old man and an old woman. After greeting us, they asked what we had to trade with them. I answered, "Linen and some salt." They said, "Bring your goods and come into our yurt." We brought our goods, and the old man brought forward felt sufficient for two outfits and placed it before us. Having put this before us, he picked up from my goods two pieces of glossy linen and placed them near the front of the yurt. As I did not know their usual ways of doing things, I asked him, "What will you give me for those two pieces of linen?" They said, "You have probably not traded in these parts before and don't know the usual ways we go about things here. I have given that felt that I put by you for these two pieces of linen. Among our people we have the habit that when we trade, we do it silently and do not ask about the price but estimate the values of things to ourselves and then make exchanges." I worked the values out to myself and considered that what he had offered me would be worthwhile and I might make a kopeck or two.

We returned to our camp, got in our boat, and again traveled up the Cholyshman using poles. When we had gone seven *versts* (five miles) from the mouth of the river, we came across five yurts and landed on the sandy bank near them. We went into the yurts and began to trade in their manner. For one sheepskin we gave about a pound of salt; for a beaver skin we gave a two-hands measure of glossy linen. While trading in this way, we went into one of the yurts belonging to the Toolos people. There were two idols inside and two women and a man sitting there. Once I had greeted them and started talking about this and that, I asked, "In this yurt here there are two women. Why are there no children? Also, there is one man here; why do you have two idols?" The man said, "I have taken two wives, but I don't have any children; I don't know whether God does not permit it or I am infertile. My oldest wife and I have made for ourselves two idols; although we use many charms, they do not seem to be of use." I asked, "What god do you believe in and call upon when you cast charms?" They answered, "When we do this we call upon our seven hills, our land and water, the father of all—Bai-Ulgen—and also Erlik." Then I told them everything, beginning with the creation of the heavens and earth right up to the last century. They listened with great attention to the account of our holy faith.

We spent six days at that place. When we were working on our boat, one of the women came every day to our place and asked questions about God and the Christian faith and listened very attentively to our answers. I talked with her every time she came. If at that time there had been a priest with us, it seems they would have been ready to be baptized. The woman said to me, "Do you baptize people?" I answered, "Only priests baptize." This woman's name was Toichin and her husband's Kuchinek. Later Toichin was baptized, and she became Natalia.

Once we had prepared the boat, we again set out, using poles to sail higher up the Cholyshman. We came to the mouth of a river called Kairylyk and spent the night there. The following day we traded with the Toolos people of the district. We spent one more night, and next day we borrowed two horses from one of the Toolos called Pyryn. My wife and I rode on them to the mouth of the Bashkaus, which joins the Cholyshman, to seek trade there. When we arrived, we found about thirty latticed yurts. At that place we traded all the rest of our goods.

Now I will tell you where the Toolos people keep all their property. They keep it in the caves among the rocks where no one ever goes. If they want to trade with you, they say, "If you want to trade with us, come back in two days and I will get ready for you the best things that we have to trade." If you ask them where they get their goods from, they answer, "Our people do not keep their things at home but keep them in mountain caves, covered with stones; we keep only the poorer things at home." When I wondered, "Why do you keep your property far away in caves?" they replied, "That is our custom and the custom of our ancestors because in the olden times, when there were wars, all the inhabitants of this region hid their goods in caves and covered them with stones. Now we still hide our goods."

Among the Toolos people of the Cholyshman region, the rich have two wives; the elder of the two stays at home and has charge of the servants while the younger one is responsible for the yard and the livestock and is also in charge of the fuel stocks and preparing the food. The elder wife sits in front, but the younger one never does.

There are tall rock-strewn mountains along the sides of the Cholyshman and Bashkaus; the pathways along the banks of both rivers are stony and very narrow, with rocky outcrops. In these mountains you may find the following wild animals: wild goats, elk, antelope, bears, lynx, wolves, deer, badgers, marmot, hare, moles, mice, rabbits, gophers, stoat, polecat, sable, otters, water mice and rats, and foxes.

There are plenty of fish in the Cholyshman, especially pike, burbot, and eel, and in the lakes above the Cholyshman it is the same. In Lake Telets there are also many fish, in particular pike, herring, giant herring, perch, and sterlet. Besides these, there are no other fish.

We put the things we had bought into three boats and set out down the Cholyshman. We stopped overnight on the bank of the lake. Later we stopped at the mouth of the river Ayu-Kechpes. We spent a day there and then went to the place where we had fished. The next day we sailed down the Biya. On our way we stopped at one place to do some fishing.

Our net caught on the some of the rough wood under the keel of our boat. I could not pull it out and became angry. So we tied the rope of the net to a tree on the bank and started to prepare a meal and brew some tea. Then I remembered how our net had been caught in the lake before and how St Nicholas helped us. In the hope that St Nicholas would help us again, I prayed within my heart, and my soul became lighter; I began to feel more cheerful and said to Yakov, "Why are we angry? He who helped us at the lake can help us now." Yakov said, "That's true— how could we forget St Nicholas?" Having said this, he, together with Stepan, jumped into the boat and rowed to the net. When they pulled, the net suddenly floated up;

then we saw that the piece of wood that had caught the net was a piece of fir with three branches. Each of the three branches had broken as if they had been cut with a saw. The biggest of them had a thickness of about 3.5 *vershki* (six inches). We looked to see whether they were rotten, but they were quite strong. Then my worker, Stepan, said, "Five men couldn't simply break a branch like this; God cut it with a saw," and he gave thanks to God. From that time to this, I have remembered what happened and made a resolution to set up a chapel in honor of St Nicholas on the bank of the lake.

We sailed further on, and when we reached the place where previously we had found the wild bees, we decided to spend the night. The next day we reached Kebezen.

PAGAN WAYS

My children! I am relating to you what life was like among the pagan peoples as I saw it in my youth. You can see what things are like in your time, so you are able to say that life in the old days was different from the present. Formerly, they were wild and ignorant. There is a saying among the old people, "*Ozo chykkan kulaktang son chykkan muus uzaar*," which means "The horns that grow later are longer than the ears that grow earlier." This saying is true, and things certainly turn out like that.

The pagan people lived in four districts: Tyurgeshck, Kuzensk, Yussk, and Komdoshsk. Their food consisted of barley, oats, and wheat. They sowed little wheat. They dried the barley and winnowed it in a trough to clear the chaff, which they blew away with a fan, and then they ground it by hand on a millstone and made it like oatmeal, mixed it with water and milk, and drank it. They also drank this with tea. They dried the wheat and oats, ground them by hand on a millstone, and made flour, which they cooked on hot ashes and then ate.

In the summer they milked the cows, heated up the milk, and then let it cool in a pan. The next day they removed the cream and put it in a leather bag made from cowhide. When it had been standing some time and had begun to turn sour, they stirred it with a stick. After this the butter rose to the top. This was removed by hand and made into blocks while the sour milk was poured into a pot and covered with a wooden lid; the gaps were sealed with clay. At the top of the lid was a hole: into this hole they put one end of a wooden tube. The gaps were filled with clay, and the other end of the tube was placed in the mouth of a jug. After this some firewood was placed under the pot. Then the boiling milk bubbled and dripped through the tube into the jug. That is how they made wine. They tested it all the time with a wooden ladle. If a lot of wine came out, then it was weak. After doing this they removed the lid from the pot and drew out the sour cream; this was put in a linen bag and hung out on a stick. By morning all the whey had drained away, and the sour cream was removed and spread out on a skin. They beat this with a brush made with hair, dried it, and made small lumps of cheese. The blocks made from butter were called *kurut*. This *kurut* was threaded on a cord and hung up to store. When they were setting out on business, they prepared *yazyk* (provisions) from these. *Aarchy* (butter blocks for a journey) were kept in a dried animal bladder, then chilled, and this together with the *kurut* was taken for provisions.

In the winter when they wanted to make provisions from animal flesh, they would take a clean bladder; stuff it with tender, pulverized meat taken from different cuts of the animal; and then freeze it. When they wanted to eat meat from this bladder, they would cut away a piece with an axe, put it into some soup with cereals, and heat it. When they heated meat, they did not heat it completely but ate it somewhat raw, and the soup, when it was cooked, was taken off the heat and allowed to cool without any covering over it. After it had cooled and the dogs began to lap it up from the pot, they beat them and chased them away. Then they ate from the same pot. When I asked why they ate what the dogs had eaten, they answered, "A dog's mouth is clean; only the hair is poisonous." Neither did they wash their hands before they ate their food. They also drank warmed animals' blood, and sometimes they poured the blood into the gut of an animal, tied both ends, heated it like that, and ate it.

When they wanted to drink wine, they dipped a finger into it, sprinkled it in front of themselves and toward the door of the yurt, and then drank. To my question,

"Why do you sprinkle the wine?" they replied, "We wish to give some to our gods—the Keeper of the Doors and Ulgen, the spirit of the earth and water—before we drink ourselves." When they were in the fields, before taking food they also sprinkled some wine toward the hills and the water. I wondered, "Why do you do that?" and they answered, "We are offering wine to the lord of the earth and water."

The clothes of the pagan people were mainly of felt. They obtained the felt from the Altai, Cholyshman, and Kemchika regions. Their footwear was specially made: the sole and tip from leather and the upper part from canvas. Although they had shoes made of soft leather, they wore them only when they were going to visit other people. When they set out on business, they wore boots with canvas tops and wrapped their legs with straw. When the wrappings became damp, they dried them before the fire.

Most of the domestic work was done by women. Even when the women were pregnant, they had to carry in the firewood. Some used a horse to drag it in. To do this they tied the timber with a rope. One of the ends was fixed to the front of the saddle, and the wood was dragged along. They did not know how to make sledges or carts. In the winter they gathered wood on skis.

They never washed their cups. When they were asked about this, they answered, "We are not in the habit of washing away the happiness that God gives us. Our people say that whoever washes cups will never have good cattle." They also said that if you wash pots and pans that have contained milk in river water, the cattle will not be happy, which meant there will be a low milk yield.

When the moon was on the wane, they would not give milk to strangers—and some would not give them milk during the new moon either. However, when someone was willing to drink it within the yurt, they would give it. That way, "the purity will not leave the yurt," as they said. Some would also not give fire to members of a strange yurt. If on the fifth day of the new moon, they were to heat and boil milk on a fire, which might be given to someone else, then they would not heat large quantities because, as they said, if the milk were to spill over into the fire, the cows would lose their milk. Some would not sell their cattle during the waning of the moon, and during the full moon they would give nothing to a stranger. If they were to hand over cattle when the moon was full, they considered that together with them would go all contentment in the cattle and they would thus become barren. When they wanted to give something to someone and that person approached them from the left-hand side, they would say, "There will be no happiness from this." When someone died, on that day they would never give anything.

When we returned from Lake Telets to Ulala, we crossed a high mountain pass with some pagan people. At the top of this pass, there were heaps of tree branches. The pagan people got off their horses, and some threw

bunches of branches onto the piles. Then they bowed low
to the piles. Seeing what they were doing, I asked, "Why
do you gather branches, bind them together, throw them
on the pile, and then bow to them?" They answered,
"Whoever doesn't put anything on the pile or bow to it
will bring bad luck to himself or to his horse; we are giving honor to the master of this mountain." I asked them,
"What is the name of the master?" They replied, "It
must be that the master of the mountain is the master of
earth and water." Some also said, "The shamans know
more about this." After we resumed our journey, I told
them about the true God who created everything, both
Heaven and earth.

They went with me as far as the Salganda settlement. I
left them there and went on to Karasuk. Near that village,
not far from the road, was a large gathering of people in an
open field. I went over to them and saw that in the middle
of the group was a young filly. One man was holding her
by the reins, and others were tying ropes to her four legs. I
got off my horse to watch. The four men pulled the filly's
legs with the four ropes in different directions. The filly
fell down onto her belly; then the people put a big pole on
her back. Many people sat on the ends of the pole. They
wound a rope around the nose and mouth of the filly and
tightened it. The filly began to suffocate, stopped breath-
ing, and gave up her life. I watched as she died and then
said, "Why do you kill an animal with such torture?"
They said, "That is how we give sacrifice to our father,

Ulgen; any other sacrifice would not be accepted." I said,
"The true God did not give such an order. God created
the horse so that people could ride it and through its help
accomplish His tasks; people should thank God for this.
It would be well for you to thank God for his generosity,
but you insult Him and offend Him by killing so cruelly
a creature He has given you. God gave the bird wings,
and when he flies he takes care of his wings. He does not
pull out the feathers, and when he gets dirty, he washes in
water. And isn't the horse, which God has given us, like
wings for man? Haven't you got the same good sense as
the birds?" They answered, "God has ordered it thus."
I insisted, "If that is so, then show me your books, and I
will look at them." But they were silent.

I spent the night on the riverbank not far from them.
The following morning I saw that they had skinned the
filly completely in one piece—from hoof to head—and
hung the hide on a long pole in an easterly direction; they
had stuffed the mouth with straw, and the legs and hoofs
were hanging down. When I saw this, I went over to the
place where they had performed the pagan ceremony and
said, "Today you have insulted God more than yester-
day." "How can that be?" they asked. "You are saying to
God, there is the horse that you gave us. We have tied it
up, suffocated it, killed it, and skinned it; now, in order to
demonstrate how evil we are, we have hung its skin from
a tree and stuffed its mouth with straw. Now look upon
our work! You should not behave this way before God.

God will come at the last times with the sun from the east to judge the living and dead. What answer will you then give to God?" They replied, "This is our custom," and went off to their yurts. I set off toward home again and at midday arrived in Ulala.

CHAPTER 3

Raising Voices and Hearts to God

For three more years, I traveled about those places, such as Cholyshman and Chern, trading in different areas. When I got home, I put my affairs in order. Earlier, when I was serving as an interpreter for Father Stepan, I sent all my daughters to learn to read and write with Sister Yevdokia. They studied with God's blessing and the support of myself and Father Stepan.

But the people of Ulala laughed at us, saying, "Chevalkov has sent his daughters to school to make them into clerks; now they will be clerks in the Bystrinsky government service and in Kokshinksy too." They spoke like this, laughing at us, especially the wealthy ones, who said, "What use is it for a woman to study?" Others said, "It is not the custom for women to learn to read and write." And still others said, "You have not taught your children needlework—who will want them?" When my wife told me about this gossip, she was upset and so I said to her,

"Both women and men are God's creations. Everyone needs to know God's laws; if we change our minds about this because we are afraid of people's adverse comments, then the devil will have the last laugh. They are not learning anything wrong: so why all this offense? Those who are laughing will weep." When I told her that God will not neglect those who study well, my wife said to me, "The nuns said that our children study very well; I am glad about that."

When Father Stepan and Mother Yevdokia started to praise our daughters to the people, others began to send their daughters to study. As a result, some of those who had laughed sent their daughters to study too. Of the people of Ulala, our daughters were the first to become literate. When they had completed their studies, I started to teach them to sing from the songbook. Every evening I gave them singing lessons, sitting on the porch in front of the house. My sisters, when they heard the singing, came and joined my daughters as well. Then I said to them, "If on some evening I am going to teach the children from the songbook, I will play on the clarinet, and when you hear the sounds of the clarinet, come and sing with us." They did as I said. As soon as they heard the sound of the clarinet, they came to me to study.

One day when I was teaching my daughters and sisters to sing, Pavel Tyudyunekov, who was passing by, complained, "Has your father or mother died as you are singing like this every evening? It is not good to hear this." I said to him, "If you don't like listening to it, then don't live here but go and live in your own place. We are singing the praises of God in our own home." He went away murmuring with discontent. Later, the Altai people murdered this Pavel Tyudyunekov because he was a rich man.

While I taught singing in the evenings, people came after work to see me. I told them about the lives of the saints in the Altai language, as they did not know Russian. At this time some students came to our mission. On Saturday evenings I went to church to pray, and there I saw one of them, reading in church, and asked the people present the name of the reader. They said, "Mikhail Andreyevich." And I thought to myself, "I must get to know him; perhaps he will be able to help me." Afterward, I did not see him for a long time. But once, after I had finished my work, I gathered the singers together and was singing with them, and I noticed that he walked by several times. I began to see him in this way every day and thought, "This reader must love singing." On another evening when we were preparing to sing, the reader went past very quietly. I invited him over: "Mikhail Andreyevich! Come over here!" He seemed to be pleased and came over and greeted us. I said, "Would you like to sing with us?" And he sang with us for an hour. After everyone had a cup of tea, they started to go home. I said, "Mikhail Andreyevich! Come to us when you hear us singing." He promised to do so, said good-bye, and went away.

From that day, whenever we gathered on my porch to sing, Mikhail Andreyevich came and joined us. After the singing, he read to us from the holy Scriptures. Eventually, he said, "As we sing from the songbook, wouldn't it be a good idea to learn some church music too?" I was pleased with this and said, "I would very much like to teach my children myself, but I do not sing it very well. You could teach them, Mikhail Andreyevich." After this he came whenever he was free to teach my children church music. My children learned very quickly and my sisters did too. I was very glad about this.

From that time Mikhail Andreyevich became a much valued friend and colleague. Before his arrival at our mission, I had often felt regret and thought, "If only some new psalm singer would come to our mission. Although we do have a few psalm singers here, they are too lazy to teach the people. For this reason the people do not sing in church. The newly baptized do not know any Russian, and because of this they feel bored when they are in church and are slack in their attendance. If only there were holy books in the Altai language!" This sadness that I felt was a sort of prayer before God. Many times I heard how my children and sisters, when they were singing, said among themselves, "It is as if God has sent us Mikhail Andreyevich." When I heard them say this, I was very glad and thought to myself, "My children clearly wish to learn."

Mikhail Andreyevich carried on teaching my family how to sing with great enthusiasm, and my children learned to sing church music very well. Then Mikhail Andreyevich said, "Now they can sing in church. I will ask Father Stepan's blessing upon their singing." I asked, "Is it acceptable for women to sing in church?" Mikhail Andreyevich said, "Everyone should sing the praises of God—both men and women." After this, Father Stepan called my children and sisters to him and gave his blessing to their singing in church. From that time they began to sing there. The fathers and mothers who had previously laughed at us now felt rather ashamed that their children were ignorant, so they started to send them to study. As for those who did not send their children to study, I went to see them and persuaded them to send their children.

Some children saw me and said, "We want to study but our parents won't allow us to. Will you please ask them for us?" So I went and asked them to allow their children to study. The numbers of those studying grew. Mikhail Andreyevich, who taught them all to sing, lived then at the school. When I went to see him, he entertained me with tea. I saw what he ate: just potatoes, nothing more. I felt sad about this and asked him to my house as a guest. This is the way we began to translate some of the holy books into Altai. He started to study the Altai language, and for nearly two years he could make no progress at all, but then suddenly he began to understand the language. I was surprised at this and said, "You could not learn the Altai language, but now it seems you have suddenly picked it all up at once." Mikhail Andreyevich answered, "The Mother of God helped me." From that time we taught singing in the Altai language.

Mikhail Andreyevich began his lessons with singing, then read the life of a saint, and finally led more singing. In this way a large number of people gathered every day, especially on feast days, when the whole schoolhouse was full. Until then, the newly baptized knew neither the teachings of the Bible nor the lives of the saints. Mikhail Andreyevich taught them with great enthusiasm, and the newly baptized, who up to that time had felt as if they were asleep, were awakened. After such hard work and study, Mikhail Andreyevich became a hieromonk. His name as a priest was Macarios. He began to teach even more than before. Together we translated many of the holy books. After a while we translated the liturgy. For more than two years, I worked on translations with him for no payment at all.

For most of the year, I was involved in trade and work in general. One day, when I had just come back from a place where I had been trading, a bishop came to Ulala and stayed at Father Stepan's house; he called me over and introduced me to the bishop. I had received the bishop's blessing and was about to leave when the bishop said, "Why don't you serve as an interpreter for the mission, Chevalkov?" I said, "The payment that I would receive for such service is not enough for food and clothing for the two of us and three daughters." He asked, "How much payment were you receiving?" I said,

"Fifty rubles." Then he said to Father Stepan, "Of course, fifty rubles is little. It must be increased." He then asked me, "If it were increased by seventy rubles, would that be enough?" I answered, "I will serve as an interpreter for one year." The bishop gave me his blessing again, and I began to work as a translator and interpreter with the monk Macarios, whom I described previously. We translated the holy books.

A WOMEN'S MONASTERY

Around this time, my children started to say to me, "We will not get married. We will serve God until death. If there was a monastery, we would go and live there." Others also expressed such a wish—in all, eleven girls. All of them were literate. I said to them, "Because you have not seen a monastery, you probably think life is easy there; you should try it first and see whether you could do it." They said, "The Mother of God would help us!"

The son of a rich man from Baiata, called Alexander, began to pay court to my middle daughter. I said to my daughter, "The son of a rich man wants to marry you. Shall I agree?" She answered, "I don't want to marry any rich man. Someday I want to enter a monastery and live there until I die." I decided I did not want to compel her. Instead, I spoke with Father Macarios [the former Mikhail Andreyevich—Ed.] about the wish the girls had several times expressed to join a monastery. Father Macarios said, "Let them test themselves beforehand and pray hard to God." Then Father Macarios taught them the morning and evening rules of prayer and showed them how to live in order to please God. They gathered in my house for prayers following the monastic rules before going to their homes. Every day their desire to serve God grew stronger. As there was only one room in my house, it became rather crowded. As a result, I bought for them a special *izba* and moved it near the mouth of the Ulala, where it flows into the Maima, so that they could have a small garden.

A year after we had set up the *izba*, men called Malkov and Suslonov brought an icon of the Mother of God to us in Ulala. They placed the icon in the church and went to Father Stepan. After drinking tea there, they said, "We took this icon to the village of Makaryevskoe and then came here to see you." Father Stepan said, "Perhaps you will decide to take it back there?" Malkov said, "We ourselves don't know. In Tomsk, Domna Karpovna [blessed Domna, a revered "fool for Christ" in Tomsk—Ed.] told us, 'This icon of the Mother of God should be taken to Mia in the Altai. It will be for them the Mother of God, their patroness.'" "Doesn't Mia mean this mission?" asked Father Stephan. And Malkov said, "That is why we have come here; we think so, too." But someone else asked, "Doesn't this mean the village of Makaryevskoe, which is not far from Mia?" Father Stepan said, "Let's go to the church and pray to the Mother of God; we will prepare two pieces of paper as lots representing two places, and after prayers we will look at the lots and know where the icon of the Mother of God should go." So they wrote out two lots for two places in the church and offered them to the icon. When they drew the lots, it came out that the icon should go to the Ulala mission.

But they did not accept this. Again they laid down lots and prayed. They looked and again the lots said Ulala. Malkov and Suslonov burst into tears and said, "May the will of the Mother of God be done." When Malkov was preparing to leave to go home, Father Macarios said to him, "Here in Ulala there are some young women; this is the second year they have devoted themselves to prayer to God." Malkov was pleased and said, "Let these girls write a letter, and when they have all signed it they can give it to me; I will put in a word for them with some important people." The eleven young women and one widow signed a letter, and Malkov sent the it to the authorities. They received their approval and a letter promising to give them some land.

The people in Ulala were angry with me because of this, and they criticized me: "What laws are you thinking up? Perhaps you want to build a monastery here and get us moved from this place? You want to take our land from us. You want to make us monastery servants. Why did you buy and move that *izba*? We don't want it set up here."

I said, "Even if they do in fact set up a monastery here, they wouldn't take your land; they would take the

land that lies over beyond yours. That is state land."
After this I piled moss halfway up the sides of the *izba*
that we had moved. One person on his own could not
place the moss any higher. It remained like this for
a month and a half, and I wanted to hire someone to
help, but those I tried to hire said that the people had
agreed to birch anyone who helped me with the moss
for the house.

While I thought about hiring someone from another
village, a document came from the authorities in Maima
that said the people from Ulala should go there because
a land surveyor was going to mark out the boundaries
between Maima and Ulala. The people of Ulala gathered together and set out for Maima. The land surveyor
said to them, "You choose from among your people a
literate person of honorable and trustworthy character.
Let him be entrusted by you to show where the boundaries of your village lie." The Ulala people could not find
such a person among themselves and said to me, "Could
we trust you to show him our boundaries? We can't find
such a person among ourselves." I answered, "I have
been of service to you many times. I am not unwilling.
But none of you has done so much for the community."
They said, "We know that you have given many services
to the community; if you have any job to do we will do
it for you, and if you don't believe it we'll give you a
promise in writing." I said, "I must cover the *izba* that I
moved with moss." They answered, "In one day we will

all get together and do it, and we will put turf on the roof too."

As a result, on that very day I set out to see the surveyor at Maima, and in one day I pointed out all the boundaries and returned home. Three days later the people gathered and covered the *izba*, including the roof, with turf. I said, "Thank you" to them. When they had gone home, I sat down and burst into tears, thinking to myself, "Truly this house is worthy of the Mother of God, for before the community forbade anyone even to work on it, but now through the goodness of the Mother of God, the people's hearts have softened and they finished off the house. God's will be done." I went home with these feelings in my heart. A week later a peasant called Tikhtovnikov came from the village of Odus-Tyobyo. I agreed that he should cover the roof with boards, and in another week, he was finished.

After work one day, when I was sitting near this house, a priest came up from the river bank and approached me. I looked at him but did not know him. He greeted me and said, "I am Father Ioann Smolyanikov." I received a blessing from him. He asked, "Why did you build a house here in this place?" I said, "Because it is better here for planting a garden." He asked, "Who gave you permission to build here?" When he said this, I immediately remembered the words of old Father Macarios a long time ago, and I said, "The previous Father Macarios told me to build here. Standing on this bank, he gave me the money." "That's fine, then," he answered.

Next, I built a stove in the house. Then the girls who had dedicated themselves to the service of God said, "We are afraid to live there alone by ourselves; we do not have an older person among us. You build a house for yourself near this one and live there, and then we will be in no danger." So I built a house for myself nearby and lived there two years. The pious girls fulfilled the rules of morning and evening prayer every day. One of my daughters was in charge of the observation of the rules; some of the girls went home after prayers and returned the following day. Two years later a nun called Anastasia came from Russia. She took charge of them and led them in the rules of prayer.

Before this nun arrived, the surveyor came to allot the land to the group. The Ulala people were offended, and at a meeting they accused me: "Out of spite you want to take a piece of land for the monastery. We'll not live here any more—we'll move." I answered them, "They won't take your land; in the document it is written that a piece of vacant land starting at Uakhta should be taken." But they would not listen to my words and shouted that they were prepared to beat me up and swore at me. I walked away from them, went back to the *izba*, and said to my wife, "I want some tea. Put the samovar on." I was very disturbed in my soul and lay down on the floor. I saw my room filling up with Altai people who were still unbaptized pagans, all in black clothes. They surrounded me and threw things at me. I was not able to move from the place but watched them, and I saw my wife preparing the samovar. At that moment old Father Macarios appeared next to me. "Why are you afraid of them? They have no power; they are weaker because they are drunk. You should simply blow them away." Then he blew on these pagans, and they all flew out of the window like hop leaves. I looked on a while longer. My wife put the samovar on the table. I asked her, "Did some Altai people come in here?" "No, they didn't come," she answered. Then I got up, drank some tea, and told her about my vision of Father Macarios. Just then, the monk-priest Father Macarios came to see me and said, "Go home and I'll come to see you soon." I left the *izba* and went back to my house. He came quickly, and we prayed to the Mother of God.

Soon after, the foreman came to me and said that the surveyor wanted me. When I tried to go in to see him, the people stopped me and said, "The community trusts you: tomorrow they will allot the land for the monastery." I was amazed and said, "I don't know anything about that. The surveyor sent for me." Then I went in, greeted the surveyor, and said, "Our community has entrusted me to represent them." The surveyor smiled and said, "Don't be angry with them. God alone knows that they have no idea what they are doing; they are mad at you about the monastery land, and yet they ask you to be their advocate.

Let them find an advocate they can trust from among themselves and not cause you such trouble. God will help them."

This surveyor ate only dry bread and water while he was marking out the land. He lived like that for three days. When I gave him a cooked meal, he ate it but said, "This is God's work. I should fast as I do it; I haven't got long to live on this earth. I have voyaged widely to worship the relics of the saints." Indeed, at night he related to me many remarkable tales. When he had drawn up a plan of the land, he sent it to the authorities. The next year, another surveyor came and set up boundary posts.

RUSSIAN EMISSARY TO CHINA

Once when the community was gathered around the porch, coming to an agreement to make me village leader, an official came to us. Getting out of his carriage, he asked the people whether there was an interpreter for the mission here called Mikhail Chevalkov. The elder, Selifon, pointed at me and said, "There he is." The official approached me and explained, "Last winter I sent you a letter from Petersburg asking you to travel to the Chinese border with me as my interpreter. Did you receive the letter?" I replied, "I have not seen any such letter." He said, "I wrote to the leader of the mission that you should not go away but stay here at home." After he said this, Andrei Gustavovich Prints, which was this official's name, took me with him to Father Stepan. There he asked, "I sent a letter requesting that Chevalkov should remain at home. Did it reach you?" Father Stepan said, "I intended to tell Chevalkov, but I was so busy that I forgot." The official said, "Let him come with me." Father Stepan answered, "At the moment he is not serving me as an interpreter. The community wants to make him village leader today." Prints asked me, "Is it true that they want to make you an elder?" I replied, "You can see that the people have met together to write the order for me to become the village elder."

The official had some tea and then summoned the village elder to him and said, "Chevalkov must be on government business with me as my interpreter and travel with me to the Chinese frontier. His name is known in Petersburg; I need him. You must write a note freeing him from the responsibilities of village elder." So the community appointed Konstantin Chevalkov as elder, and two days later, I set out with Prints.

At first we observed and collected information on the Kumandinsky and Chernevy native peoples; on the overnight stops I took the opportunity to tell them about the holy Scriptures. From there we went along the banks of the Bii River until we reached Kebezeni; we spent a day there and then set out along Lake Telets, where we spent the night at Artuash. The official said, "What are you telling these people about?" I answered, "About God." And he replied, "If you feel up to it, go ahead. This is no bad thing to do."

From there we went on further by boat. We spent two more nights on the journey before we reached the mouth of the Cholyshman, where it enters the lake.

At Kyrsae, seven Soyonts people were trading. [The Soyonts people at that time were subjects of the Chinese Empire.—Ed.] They told us, "We've been here seven days. The people here will not allow us to go further." At Kyrsae a Chinese official had forgotten to fix a boundary stone but said, "I have renewed the boundary here. No person can pass this place from Russian territory to our land without a pass." "We want to go back home now," insisted the Soyonts people.

My official said, "If they do not allow us and these people to pass, then how shall we proceed? It seems they will not give us permission." I answered, "I'll find a way to get through; tomorrow in the morning we will leave here by climbing higher." The official said to me, "Don't upset them. By the looks of them they are unpleasant people." I answered, "No, they are a timid and peaceful people. I have spent some time with them before."

By this time about thirty Toolos people had gathered. I said to them, "Let us through." They answered, "Where are you going?" "We are going to the upper waters of the Chui," I replied. They said, "An important official came from China, an *albyn* [senior Chinese civil servant—Ed.]. He marked out this land and said that from the mouth of the Cholyshman and beyond was out of bounds to Russians; the boundary marker that he fixed is here at

Kyrsae." I asked them, "Was there a Russian official with him?" They answered, "No, there were only Chinese officials and some Kurgany." I said, "If that is the case, then they have stolen the land of the White Tsar. Usually two emperors divide the land between them. Therefore, there should be an official present from the White Tsar. How can the Chinese *albyn* by his own authority slice off a piece of land belonging to the White Tsar?" They answered, "The *albyn* has documents concerning the allocation of land: one document is with the junior official at Toargi on the Cholyshman, and the other is with the *demich* [junior official—Ed.], Somokaka, who lives at Koo." I said, "Send people to get these documents." They sent someone, and we drank tea and lay down to sleep.

In the morning we looked around and there were even more people gathered than before. I went up to them, and they said, "They brought the documents in the night. Will you look at them now?" I took the papers in my hand, glanced at them, and took them to our camp. When I got there, I sat down, studied them, and then put them in my pocket. In a little while, they came after me and asked, "Have you read the papers?" I said, "I have read them." They asked, "What is written on them?" I said at random, "It says nothing in these papers about the allocation of territory, but it does say that carts should be prepared with supplies and that the people should be ready and wait here." Then they said, "We are illiterate. How could we know that?" When they asked me to return the papers, I replied, "I will not give them to you for they are false papers. Now we will go to the upper reaches of the Chui and show them to the *zaisan*'s clerk." [A *zaisan* is a local administrative official in the Altai region.—Ed.]

During this conversation, Andrei Gustavovich Prints came out of the tent and asked, "What were you talking about?" I told him everything we had said. He asked, "Aren't you going to give the papers back to them?" When I did not hand them back, they went back to their camp, and we sat down and drank tea. My official said to me, "If they don't go along with that, we won't fight about it. We'll go back by the lake." I said, "You'll see, they won't attack me. They are a peaceful people." Then I called them to us, and they all came over. My official was a young man, and he went into the tent. I said to the Toolos people, "Will you give us a cart?" "We are afraid to give you our master's carts." I said, "You live on the territory of the White Tsar, and you plow his land. If you do not give a cart to the official who has been sent by the White Tsar, then we, without leaving this place, will send a paper to Biysk. If they send armed forces from there, what will you do?" They answered, "We are afraid that our master, the *albyn* watching the boundary, will blame us for letting a Russian official go by." Then I said to them, "You won't be guilty, but your master the *albyn* will be guilty for marking out the boundary without having orders for this from the two emperors." After this I called over Antonov, Luchshev, and the two

Tuzikov brothers with some workers who were traveling to the Soyonts people to trade, and together we threw aside the boundary marker.

The Toolos were silent, and I said, "Prepare the carts quickly!" They quickly prepared the carts and slaughtered a black sheep to provide supplies for us. We had a meal and then set out. In three days we reached Kosh-Agach. The carriers working for us were poor people, so when we stopped at night, I gave them sugar, and they were very pleased with me. When I asked them, "Has your *albyn* received many presents from the people?" They answered, "He took about seventy horses and a lot of foxes and sables." I asked, "What did he say? Why did he take these?" They replied, "He said that it was because they had taken over our land."

We spent the night at Kosh-Agach. All the Chuisk elders and important people came to see us and set up their camp near ours. My official said to me, "Let's go to the *zaisan*'s yurt." I asked the community for some horses and set out with the official to Zaisan Chichkan's yurt.

Zaisan Chichkan entertained us with tea. After we sat for a while, I raised the question of the boundary markers that the *albyn* had set up in Kyrsae. The *zaisan* said, "When he was here, that *albyn* plundered the local people and nearly ruined them. He said that some new law had been published."

I said, "You would do better to give your allegiance to the White Tsar than be exposed to exploitation by the Chinese." The *zaisan* said, "If the White Tsar would accept us, then we would willingly transfer ourselves to his authority." I answered, "This land on which you are living belongs to the White Tsar; for this you pay him *kalan* (a form of local tax). It would be better for you to pay one tax than two. That *albyn*, once he has found you, will want to plunder your people every year." The *zaisan* answered, "Tomorrow I will gather together all the best and most important people and come with them to your camp so you can talk to them."

After that conversation, we returned to spend the night at our camp. A lot of people came to see us the next day, and Zaisan Chichkan was with them. My official did not come out of the tent: he was writing reports. I explained the *albyn*'s deceit to those who had gathered near us, and in conclusion I said, "Every day the *albyn* and the Yurgans by deception gather up to forty head of cattle from the Cholyshman region for their supplies. Out of these they consume only three, and they sell the rest to the Chinese people who live near there. Isn't this behavior of theirs ruinous to you? They have taken about seventy horses from the Cholyshman people, promising to give them land, and on top of that they have taken a lot of foxes and sable. Does this show the *albyn*'s consideration for you? They want to clean you out and then hand you over naked, except for your souls, to the White Tsar. You write out everything the *albyn* has done with you, and send it to his superiors. Then you will know all about what is true and what is false."

Then they said, "We will discuss this among ourselves." They made a fire with a small willow tree and sat down for a long time to talk over the problem. Meanwhile, my official called me over to drink tea. He said to me, "What were you talking about?" I told him everything I had said to them. The official asked, "Have they agreed?" And I replied, "They have gathered together over there to decide." After drinking my tea, I went over to the place where they were sitting. They said, "If the White Tsar does not accept us, then we'll end up guilty before two masters." I said, "But the land where you live belongs to the White Tsar; therefore, what have you to fear? If you give your word to be loyal to him, this official will send to the emperor a document; then the two emperors can discuss it among themselves." They said, "Whatever will be, will be. We will transfer our allegiance to the White Tsar," and all of them shook my hand.

Then I went over and told my official, "They have given me their hand that they will transfer their allegiance to the White Tsar." The official smiled when he heard this and said, "So they want to transfer?" He did not say more.

After spending one more night there, we reached the boundary marker at Sook in one day. There we met an official and passed the night. The next day, on the return journey, we spent the night on the road. On the fourth day we arrived at Yailyaush. From there it took two days to reach Kairylyk. When I was preparing to go home from Kairylyk, my official gave me sixty-seven rubles.

During the next year at home, I was busy with blacksmiths' work. One day, a paper came to me from the governor. When I had taken hold of the paper, Father Akakii came up to me and said, "The governor wrote that paper in my presence in Biysk. He is ordering you to go to the village of Altaisk and wait for him there. He wants to have you with him as an interpreter when he goes to Kosh-Agach. You had better go there quickly tomorrow morning. In the paper it says that a cart will be available to you." Therefore, on the next day I went there and waited at the apartment where Governor Lerkho would stay.

The governor came within an hour. He got out of his carriage and went into the house. Soon he came back out and asked the people around, "Is Chevalkov here?" I said, "Here I am." He said, "Come here." When I went up to him, Governor Lerkho greeted me, took my hand, and led me into the room. There he said to me, "Last year did you go to Kosh-Agach?" I replied, "Yes, I went with Prints." He smiled and said, "You took two districts under control, and now we must go there. Once we have confirmed this, we can put it in writing. You are needed as an interpreter. Do you have any spare clothes with you?" I said, "Yes, I have brought some." "Excellent," he replied.

Later we set out, and in two days we reached Ongudai. A large number of Altai people and their *zaisans* had gathered in the street. The Governor Lerkho said to me, "These two men are involved in some sort of legal case between them. Go over and see if you can find out what they are arguing about. The *zaisans* are there—let them listen. When you have worked out what's going on, come and tell me." I had only just gone out into the street when the local official interpreter, Karbyshev, went over to the people and said to the *zaisans*, "The governor has ordered that this interpreter, Chevalkov, should sort out these legal disputes. Where are Taak and Kurman Chernov? Let Chevalkov sort out their problem."

After hearing the details of their argument, I found Kurman Chernov the guilty party and awarded six horses to Taak. Then I found the governor and told him about what had happened. Governor Lerkho went out and asked the *zaisans*, "Are you satisfied with the outcome of this business?" The *zaisans* answered, "We approve." So the governor said, "Write out a document for me then, stating that you approve of the outcome." They wrote it and fixed their seals on it.

We left Ongudai and in four days reached Kosh-Agach, where we stayed at Gilev's house. On the road I felt worried in my heart: "What if the Chui *zaisans* refuse and say that they did not give their word to transfer their allegiance to the White Tsar. That would look bad for me!" I felt very fearful.

When we arrived at Kosh-Agach, the Chui *zaisans*, their leading citizens, and the community as a whole were gathered together. Governor Lerkho got off his horse, asked me to stand beside him, and said, "Do you recognize this man?" They said, "We have seen him many times." The governor said, "What did he tell you last year?" They replied, "He told us that we should transfer ourselves to the White Tsar." The governor then asked, "And you promised to transfer?" And they answered, "If the White Tsar will accept us, then we will transfer. We shook hands over this with the interpreter." The governor inquired, "Do you still want to transfer?" "We want to," they assured us. Then the weight on my mind lessened, and I felt very pleased. Governor Lerkho said to the chairman, Sudovsky, "You make a list of all these people, and ask the *zaisans* to add their seals." The next day, one of the Yurgans, who had deceived the Chui people by promising allocations of land for them, did not arrive when he was supposed to. He had hanged himself on the way!

The following morning, I saw that some Chinese soldiers had built up a stone embankment, and they were praying by it. They prayed for about half an hour. Afterward, when the governor saw me, he said, "What did you see in your dreams today, Chevalkov?" I replied, "I didn't see anything in my dreams, but I did see some Chinese soldiers build an embankment of stones and say prayers by it."

Later Governor Lerkho invited all the Russian merchants to drink tea and said to them, "How many years have you been trading here and yet you have no chapel where you can go to give praise to God? A church must be built here. Talk it over among yourselves and build one. Do you see the Mongol pagans, following their faith, setting up shrines, and saying prayers while we, who profess the true faith, should be ashamed of ourselves before these pagan people? I will give some money toward the foundation of a church, and you collect the rest among yourselves and build one!" After this, by subscription each one gave as much as he could. Gilev promised to organize the construction and to make up for what was lacking from his own pocket. In this way a church was built in Kosh-Agach.

We spent three days there, and on the fourth day we climbed along the river Yal-Agash. When we reached the summit, we saw that the whole valley from mountain to mountain was covered with thick ice. Along this ice there was a roadway, strewn with earth. Although it was midsummer and the days were hot, the ice did not melt. As we were crossing this ice, we saw in one place a large hole. Leaving my horse with one of the guides, I went over to have a look at it, and it seemed that the thickness of the ice in this hole was about five *arshin* (8 feet) and the gap beneath the ice twenty *sazhen* (120 feet). Trees without any bark could be seen at the bottom of this space: larches and fir. I asked the locals, "When does this ice melt?" They answered, "Even our ancestors have never seen it melt. It seems it must have been like this for hundreds of years." Governor Lerkho said, "In former times it was warmer here, and as a result the trees grew; now every year the surface of the ground is getting colder. In a thousand years or so, the river Chui will become ice that will not melt in the summer."

We went on. In another place there was a hole in the ground. Here, there was no depth in the soil; the thickness of the layer of earth was about one *arshin* (two feet) and beneath that was ice of a thickness of an *arshin*. On the surface of the ground was green grass. Under the ice was nothing but rock. The governor explained, "The gap between the soil and the rock was filled with water in the summer. This water lifted the soil upward. When the frost came, the water turned to ice; when it grew warm again and the layer of ice that was under the soil melted and became water, it flowed away. For this reason a gap appeared. Now the ice that remains will never melt."

After this we went to Azh, a mountain pass. Here, I saw glaciers fed by the frozen mountains. The largest of these glaciers was the height of a hill. Crossing the pass, we dropped down into Yazadyr. From there we descended and reached a small river called the Adagan, which we crossed using poles. Further on, we crossed the river Koks on horseback and spent a night there. Then we spent a night in the midst of bushes that grew by the lower reaches of the little river Arzhan. After leaving this place, we spent the next night at the village of Fykulka.

The following day, the governor gave me seventy-six rubles and I returned home.

Shortly after this trip with the governor, an opportunity arose to do something I had waited to do for a long time. Years ago, when I was working as an interpreter for Father Stepan, many unbaptized people lived on both banks of the smaller rivers that flowed into the Maima from both sides. When I asked him if I might go and spend time with them and teach them about the true God, he said to me, "I will be needing you, but one day when we are free we will both go there." For many years, though, we did not find the opportunity to go to them. In my mind, I found this very disturbing.

BAPTIZING AMONG THE YURTS

Soon after I returned from Kosh-Agach, a man came to me from the upper reaches of the Maima, where the people were unbaptized, and said to me, "The elders Motko and Tabyshtu have asked you to come and vaccinate their children against smallpox." I told Father Stepan that they had sent for me. Father Stepan gave me his blessing for my journey, and I set out with great joy to answer their call. When I was there, I went around to all the yurts and gave the vaccinations and at the same time told them about Jesus Christ, the true God. When I went round again to see that the vaccinations were satisfactory, I told them the same thing again. Soon after, Tabyshtu's children were baptized and then the wife of Tarbagan and her two sons. Motko remained unbaptized until his death, but those people who lived lower down the river from him were all baptized.

The following year, a man came to me from Karasuk and also asked me to go there to give the vaccinations. My horse happened to be somewhere in the fields, and I was too lazy to look for him, so I went to Karasuk on foot. There again I went around to all the yurts, gave the vaccinations, and explained the teachings of the true God. The local people gave me a horse, and on this horse I went to the village of Ynyrga, vaccinated the people there, and spoke of God to the people I met on my travels. When I went to Karasuk on another occasion, I did the same. As a result, during the following summer many people were baptized, for whenever I went to see them in response to their requests I told them about the holy faith. I hope it pleased God that these travels of mine were not in vain. Now, only a few of the local people there are unbaptized.

On yet another occasion, I went to Karasuk to do some fishing. I entered the yurt of one unbaptized person called Kadik. A large number of unbaptized people were sitting there. When he saw me, Kadik remarked, "You're already starting to go gray!" I said to him, "If man did not age, and horse did not waste away, then Heaven would not tremble and earth would not be destroyed." Kadik asked, "How does Heaven tremble and the earth become destroyed?" I answered, "In the last times, all creation will change. The true God, Jesus Christ, will come to earth to judge the living and dead and send his holy angels. Then they will float in the air and blow their trumpets: the earth will be destroyed, the heavens will tremble, and all creation will change." Kadik wondered, "There is nothing stronger than stone. Will that change too?" I said, "Who created fire?" "God created it," replied Kadik. "Do you think that God, who created this fire that can heat up stones and turn them to ashes, does not have command over stone? If God created it, then He can do what He likes with it. He can do all things. He made all of creation out of nothing. He said, 'Let this be,' and it was as He wished. In the last times, it will be as He says it will be. And whatever He does not will, will not be." Kadik fell silent, and I began to tell him about the creation of Heaven and earth and all that is in them, right up until the last days. I told him too about the sufferings of the unbaptized and sinners, of the blessed state of those who believe in Christ and keep His commandments, and how this blessed state will continually grow in the new world. The people who were sitting around me listened with great attention. After Kadik heard everything I had to say, he requested that his children be baptized.

Once more I went to some of the unbaptized, this time to those who lived at Syuult. There were thirteen yurts there. I went round these yurts and preached about the true God. It was evening, so I stayed the night, and the next day I went round again and preached the Gospel. The inhabitants said, "We can't get our minds around this, but we will give it some thought." I went back home but could not get them out of my mind, so I went again to speak to them. This time they said, "At the moment we are busy, but when we have finished our summer work, we will come down to Ulala to be baptized." But for two years, they did not come.

For this reason I went to see them again. I stayed two days and talked with them about God, beginning with the creation of the world right up to recent times. The next day, after I had prayed to God, I gathered them together in one place and said to them, "I have told you many times about the true God. You have all heard what I have said. Whoever has heard and not believed and given his trust to God is seriously guilty. What can justify such people on this earth? To you, God will say, 'I sent My man who knows Me and My teaching to you: you have heard from him My name and My teachings, and you have also heard of My grace. Why did you reject Me? Did I not create you? Why do you hate Me?' How will you answer God then? And what if God tells you, 'I came down from Heaven in order to raise you to Heaven. I gave Myself over to suffering in order to redeem you from eternal suffering: I was three days with the dead in order to free you from eternal death and torture under the power of the devil; I suffered on earth so that you might dwell in Heaven and so that on this earth you might rejoice and live a life of blessings; I submitted myself to slander in order to open for you the glories

of Heaven; and I lived on earth with no place to rest
my head so that you might become citizens of Heaven.
I poured out my own blood to purify and cleanse you
of your sins. Why did you despise such gracious kindness from me? I loved you more than a mother loves her
children, and you gave no thought to me when you were
mortal in the flesh. Now, you who are accursed, go from
me to Gehenna and terrible suffering.' And what will
you do then?"

Now several of them said, "Perhaps we will believe in
God and be baptized. You come here with a priest; anyone among us who wishes to will be baptized." So I sent
a letter to Ulala, and the next day Father Ioann came. He
baptized about twenty people then, but later the others
were also baptized.

After this I went to some unbaptized people who lived
at a place called Emeri and told the people who lived there
about the true God. In the course of three years, they were
all baptized. In addition, I persuaded Kochkoran and his
sons to be baptized, along with their children. I was the
godfather to his sons. The oldest son, Vasilii, said to me,
"I don't have any horses, and my gun is with a man called
Kaak, who lives at Parkynaye. I can't get there; please,
Godfather, give me a horse to get there." I asked him,
"Are there many people living there?" Vasilii replied,
"There are more than ten yurts at that place." Then with
great joy I said, "I'll go with you." He was very pleased
and said, "If you go with me, he will be afraid and won't

make difficulties about giving me back my gun." The next day I set out to see Kaak at Parkynaye.

There were many yurts, and in the course of the day I went round them all and spoke to the inhabitants about God, beginning with the creation of Heaven and earth and continuing right up to the present. People followed me from yurt to yurt. Toward evening I came to the yurt belonging to Koordek Poi, where Kaak was living, and I spent the night there. Kaak, who was expected to pay for Vasilii's gun, did not have the money, so we agreed that he would live with and work for me as payment. The following day I went with Kaak back to Ulala. Every day I talked a little with him. Listening to me, he said, "I would like to believe in God, but what shall I do if my bride, who is betrothed to me, refuses to be baptized? I have been working for my future father-in-law for hardly any payment for twelve years." I said to him, "If she refuses to be baptized, then we will get back some payment for your work." When Kaak was baptized, he was given the name Arsenii.

Soon after this I went to see the bride to whom Kaak was betrothed and said to her, "Kaak has been baptized for the love of God. Now I have come for you." She said, "I didn't tell him to be baptized, and I won't be baptized myself." Therefore, I asked for payment from the father because Kaak had worked for him for twelve years. Altaichy, the bride's father, said, "I am a poor man. What could I pay him with? However, if I were to be baptized, then my daughter would be baptized and marry the man to whom she is betrothed." I said, "Tell all your brothers, too, that they should be baptized." Altaichy gathered all his brothers together. During the night I told them about the grace of God, about the wonderful light in which those who have been baptized will dwell, and about the terrible tortures that await the unbaptized. They listened to all this with interest.

The following day twelve men set out with me for Ulala. After teaching them prayers for two days, Father Akakii baptized them. Then he went to Parkynaye to baptize the women and children who had stayed at home. The rest of the people there were baptized during the next year, and not one single person remained unbaptized. There were about fifty people baptized in all.

Another time, I set out to look for bees in the valley near some yurts on the upper reaches of the Ulala. As I found a small wood with bees in it, I decided to spend the night in the yurt of Kaibash, who had not been baptized. There were five yurts nearby. I went round to all of them and told the people about God. One orphan, Taduzhek by name, expressed a desire to be baptized, and I took him to Ulala. Following his lead, about twenty people were soon baptized, and within two years all the rest had been baptized too.

When Father Macarios Nevsky was in Chemalye, I joined him to translate the Gospels and some psalms. I was lying on the floor one evening, talking with Father

Macarios, when I saw three men come through the door. Putting a book to my mouth, they said, "This is very sweet. Eat it." I ate it up from one corner to the middle, and they said to me, "It is good that you have eaten it." Then they left, and I watched them but could not speak, and Father Macarios, who was in bed, said something to himself. When the three men gave me the book to eat, I could see the window and Father Macarios, but to this day I cannot say whether I was asleep or awake at the time. Since then I have always wondered about it.

I stayed in Chemalye for about a month. Father Macarios taught the children to read and write every day, and for about an hour he taught them church singing. When he was giving a service in the church, the children were not able to sing properly because they had no one to lead them. Father Macarios said to me, "Bring your own children to live here for a month or so; the local children can sing with them and learn from them." So I brought my wife and children, and they spent about a month there. When haymaking time arrived, we all returned to Ulala, and the children of Chemalye began to sing on their own. After haying season was over, I went there again on my own.

Around this time, Father Vladimir became leader of the mission and came to live in Ulala, and I served him as an interpreter. Many times I went with him to Altai, Chui, and Cholyshman. I translated Father Vladimir's talks on the true God to the pagans. Every year the number of those who had been baptized increased. He also gave a lot of help to the poor.

With his permission, in my free time, I went fishing. Once I was fishing on the upper reaches of the Maima. There I met a man with graying hair, and after we exchanged greetings, I asked his name. "My name is Tiskenek," he answered. "Where do you live?" I inquired, and he explained, "We lived very happily in Choposh, but now sadly we live in Karagol." I wondered aloud, "Why did you leave a place where you were happy and move to a place where you are unhappy?" He answered, "We were forced to move. We had a place where our fathers lived happily for centuries, but then Russian *chashechniki* (dissenters) arrived. They fought with us and drove us away; they also took our pastures and hay fields." I said, "Whoever weeps from such offenses will rejoice in the future; he will rejoice when he seeks God's help and gains it." Tiskenek said, "They have built themselves houses, so what can we do now?" I replied, "They have deceived the officials who are responsible for this land, as if Choposh were an empty place with no one living there. Isn't that what happened?" Tiskenek answered, "How can I know? If only we could find a way to chase them off!"

I said, "If God helps, we will find a way." Tiskenek responded, "What could be better than the help of God? But where is such a God?" I told him, "The true God is merciful and loves mankind. He is Jesus Christ, who accepts the prayers of the just and comforts those who have been hurt." Tiskenek answered, "How can we pray if we do not know the name of the true God, and how can we ask Him for help?" I explained, "If you were baptized, then you would know. There are priests, sent by God, who care for the souls of all people. They want to help people, to help those who have been hurt, to give peace to their souls, to calm those who weep, and to prepare their souls so that at their deaths they will be pleasing to God." Looking up to Heaven, Tiskenek promised, "Lord God, if You will favor us, we will be Yours." I said, "Tell your brethren what I have said," but Tiskenek warned, "They will not believe my words; you yourself must come and repeat it to them." I replied, "You tell the older priest who is the leader of the mission, and he will send me to your yurts."

After I got home from fishing, I went to the archimandrite and told him what I had heard. The father gave me his blessing and, taking two of my children who could sing with me, I set out for Karagol. There were twelve families there. I put my tent near them and prepared to stay for a while, but none of the local people came near us. Each day I tried to visit them in their yurts, but the elders were never at home. At this time they were reaping corn, and they always returned home very late. The next day they would get up very early and set out for the fields. Many days passed like that, and I was not able to see them and speak with them. Our supplies got low, so we gathered mushrooms, cooked them, and ate them. My children felt like crying with longing to go home.

But eventually, we made a little progress. One evening when we were singing in the Altai language a song called "The Truth Is All We Need," a boy came up and sat near the fire and listened. We gave him a bit of sugar. The next day three boys came, and we gave them tea with sugar. On the third day, a woman came with the three boys. I spoke with the woman about the true God and His mercy.

The following day, Tiskenck came and asked, "It seems you have been staying here a while. Have you seen my brothers?" I said, "I came here some time ago, but everyone comes back from the fields very late, and in the morning they go again to the fields. So I have not been able to see and speak to them." Tiskenek told me, "We have a brother called Kalanak; we listen to him, whatever he says. He is at home ill: go and see him and tell him all about God and the true faith. If he chooses to believe in God and is baptized, then all twelve families here will believe in God." Then Tiskenek set out for the fields.

We had enough provisions left for only one more day. Following Tiskenek's advice, I went to Kalanak's yurt. He was ill and lying down. When he saw me, Kalanak got up from his bed. I exchanged greetings with him, and he said, "It seems you've been staying here more than ten days; for what reason have you been staying here for such a long time?" I answered, "I am not here for my own reasons but have put up with cold and hunger for the sake of the people here. Now I have provisions left for only one day. I came here to do a good favor for the people, but they get back from the fields too late at night and in the morning they leave again too early for me to help them." Kalanak asked, "Did you come here to do some good for us? Did the elders send you?" I explained, "The archimandrite sent me; he said to me that in Karagol he could hear the cries of God's sheep who have lost their homes, and he sent me here so that the devilish wolf should not deceive them and that after their deaths they should not descend into the torments of the fiery pit. He sent me so that I could tell them this in their native Altai language."

Kalanak said, "I heard about the true faith from Father Macarios of Chemalye, who can speak the Telyeut language. Tell me more about the true God." He lay down again and listened to me while I told him as much as I could about the true God and about the true faith. Then Kalanak called all his brothers together and announced, "This man, together with his children who can read and write, came here for our sakes. He has put up with hunger here and has come to us not to do us any harm but for the good of our souls and ourselves. We give to the devil the cattle that God has given us. When the policeman comes from the authorities, we slaughter a two-year-old calf for him. The same police beat some of us with whips, and if they see anything of value they take it, but these people who have come here for our good are starving among us. Slaughter from our herd a three-year-old calf and also give him your word that you will believe in God. Don't set yourself up against this by saying, 'we won't believe in God'; things will go badly for us after such a promise."

After hearing Kalanak's opinion, the people brought a three-year-old calf, slaughtered it, and gave me their word that they would be baptized. I wrote down everything that happened and everything I heard and sent it to the archimandrite. The next day, the monk Ivan Vasilievich (Solodchin), Yakov Stepanovich (Koninin), and the *feldsher* (assistant doctor) Aleksei Dmitrievich (Voinov) brought us plenty of provisions, so instead of despair, we now felt great joy. After suffering hunger, we now had an abundance of good food. Every day we sang the praises of God, and every day the local people came after they had finished work to learn how to pray. As we taught them to pray, we told them about the true faith. Six days later, the father archimandrite came. There were also many people from Chemal and Ulala. In the course of three days, sixty-three people were baptized, and those living in another place nearby were baptized later. As a result, the peasants from Choposh returned to their old homeland, and some of the newly baptized bought *izby* from them and began to live with them. Father Macarios also went to live there. He taught them about the faith and taught their children reading and writing. Soon, they built a church. Those who lived near Choposh and had not been baptized were also brought to the true faith.

For a time, I joined Father Macarios in Choposh and helped him. On one visit, while I was teaching the local people, I reprimanded a certain old man for something he had done wrong. When I got home, I lay down on the floor to rest a little. As I was dozing, I saw someone standing beside me, who said, "You are a young man. Why do you rebuke and humiliate a person older than you? From this time do not behave in this way to those older than you." Then he disappeared. I immediately got up from the place where I was lying and looked all around the *izba*; when I could not find anyone, I went out onto the street, but there was no sign of anyone there either. I was amazed. Just as I went back into the house, Father Macarios arrived. After I told him what I had heard, he brought a book and showed it to me. I read it and recognized that it was one of St Paul's epistles. There, it is written, "Do not reproach and speak scandal of those older than yourself." I have never forgotten it.

On another occasion, I went to Choposh and spent three days working with Father Macarios on the translation of the holy Scriptures. Again while I was resting on the floor, I saw the monk Ivan Vasilievich Solodchin standing by my feet. At that moment, I could not move from my position on the floor or speak. He said to me, "Come quickly back to Ulala. We will teach the pupils together from the holy Scriptures, and you can learn something from this yourself." Then he left. Once he was gone, I jumped up, followed him into the street, and looked around, but there was no one to be seen and I knew that Ivan Vasilievich was in Ulala. Two days later, I went back to Ulala. The day after my return, the archimandrite said to me, "It is a good thing you have come back because tomorrow Ivan Vasilievich will be explaining the holy Scriptures to the pupils, and you should listen too—you will learn something." Even now I am still amazed at what I saw in Choposh.

MIRACLES NEVER CEASE

In the spring of that year, archimandrite Vladimir said to me as he was setting out for Russia, "Don't cease doing what you have been doing so far. God will not desert you; He will sustain you, and the rewards for God's work will be without price." After he said this, he gave me his blessing and set out. Several of the newly baptized were in tears as they parted from him.

Shortly after this, Father Macarios too set out for Russia, and several of the newly baptized asked me, "Where did Father Macarios go?" I told them, "He has gone to Russia." [He went in 1867 to St Petersburg to prepare the first Altai primer, which was published in 1868.—Ed.] Some of them were in tears as they said, "Now that he has left us too, who will teach and lead us?" As I watched their tears, I could not restrain myself and I too wept.

When Father Macarios and the archimandrite left, I was working on the translation of the lives of the saints, but I had received no money for it recently, and I was very worried because my family had little to eat or drink. On top of that, every day my wife grumbled at me, saying, "You stayed with the priests without thinking of yourself and giving yourself no rest, and now you are perishing with hunger. Isn't it a sin that you are leaving your children to cry and go hungry?" Such daily grumbling caused me more sorrow than the hunger itself. While I was suffering like this, the Feast of Pascha was approaching. My wife said, "It's only three days to Pascha. Tell me, will you rejoice or weep at Pascha? At Pascha people rejoice and enjoy themselves, but with the children we will suffer and be in great need." I said, "Whoever weeps, will later rejoice and be glad."

Two days before Pascha, I was looking out of the window and feeling very depressed. Just then, a gray-bearded old man came up to our gate and got out of his sledge. I went out to greet him, and he said, "I have brought you some wheat flour. Where shall I put it?" I asked, "Who sent me this flour?" He replied, "I have brought you some of my own flour." I asked, "You sell flour? For how much?" He answered, "For seventy kopecks." I suggested, "You must be cold. Let's go into the house." He went into the house and sat down by the door, and I invited him to have a cup of tea with us. He said, "I don't drink tea," so I offered him something else, and while we were drinking, no one spoke. After sitting quietly for a while, he said, "Where shall I put the flour? Let's go and get it." But I told him, "I haven't any money. What can I give you?" He answered, "I don't want money now; I'll get it later." We weighed the flour and stored it away. There were seventeen poods (272 pounds). I said, "Let's go into the house and get warm again; we will talk together there." I went inside and sat down by the window, but he got in his sledge and left. I ran after him and asked what his name was, and he said, "Gerasim." He said nothing more and hurried away, while I remained standing in wonder. He never came back for the money. Many years have passed since then, but I've never forgotten what happened, and I still wonder at it.

The next day, on the eve of Pascha, Alexander Stepanovich Koninin, a local resident, brought us more than a pood of beef (thirty pounds), and with thanks to God we celebrated Pascha with great joy and happiness. And just as the flour that Gerasim brought began to run out, a state assessor called Borisov asked if he could find lodging with us. I offered, "If you want to take the first floor and will pay me eight silver rubles for it, then you can certainly live with us." So he moved in, and we no longer lacked the means to buy food. Soon after I also received forty silver rubles sent by Father Macarios from Russia and then another forty silver rubles sent by Archimandrite Vladimir. My wife was overjoyed. Seeing her happiness I said, "Didn't I tell you that whoever works for God will not die of hunger? Do you see this now?" Then I taught her more about God and His saints.

For twenty-five years I worked as an interpreter for the mission and translated the holy Scriptures into the Altai language. For this in 1863 I received an award of a gold medal from the blessed emperor Alexander Nikolayevich. I continued to serve as an interpreter for another six years, and in the seventh year His Holiness Platon, bishop of Tomsk and Semipalatinsk, said to me when he came to Ulala, "Tomorrow at the service I shall consecrate you a deacon; prepare yourself." When I heard these words I left, feeling a sort of unworthiness, and returned home in tears. In such a state the chippings on the roadway appeared to me to be huge. When I got home, my wife asked, "Why are you weeping?" I answered, "Tomorrow the bishop wants to make me a deacon." I went to the window and wept, leaning my hands against the frame. My wife said, "You're being foolish. What are you looking at there? Do you want to run off into the fir trees? Pray and ask God for help, and He will help you." But instead I thought to myself, I have no outer cassock and cassock. How can these be made up in one day? The bishop won't wait; he has to leave soon. Then I had another thought: will I remain the same as I was?

Just then, a merchant came into my yard and unharnessed his horses. Soon Father Macarios came too. He bought some black cloth from the merchant, and as he gave it to me he said, "Let your children sew for you a cassock from this. Tomorrow you will need it." I could not say anything in response. More or less at the same time,

one of my pupils came to me and said, "The archimandrite wants to see you." When I went to the archimandrite, he gave me an outer cassock. Like a man whose
hands and legs have been unbound, I returned home.

Within an hour, Ivan Vasilievich gave me a hat,
saying, "A deacon needs to wear a hat; you'll need this
tomorrow." Then I began to think to myself, is it true that
you cannot run away from the destiny God has chosen for
you? In the evening I read about the order of the service,
and in the morning I got up early and read it again. Then
I went to the service, and there they made me a deacon.
The grace of the Holy Spirit overwhelmed me. Within
another seven years, I was made a missionary priest. And
two years later, I received a shield and a hat.

That same year, they sent me to Cholyshman to do
missionary work. In the six days I was there, I visited all
the yurts and got to know all the unbaptized people. I
told them about God and our true holy faith. My work
there was not in vain. With God's help, many started to
believe. In the course of ten years, one thousand became
servants of the true God. Some had been oppressed by illnesses inspired by the devil, but after they were baptized,
they were completely cured. Some of them were bound
hand and foot with other illnesses, but the strength of
God broke the bonds of the devil, and to this day they are
completely healthy. The unbaptized, on seeing the kindness and power of God, turned to God with firm faith
and were baptized. At times of illness they organized

prayers to St Panteleimon and the Mother of God. Sometimes, hindered by the great distance from a priest, large groups of people would gather and pray together for the sick, and God mercifully accepted their firm faith and prayers. Sometimes the sick recovered that very same day. If the sick person did not recover with one or two days, they knew that the day of his end was near and sent for the priest. I rejoiced on seeing that their faith was so firm.

For two years in Cholyshman I taught the newly baptized all that they needed to know: I taught them to make sleighs, to construct carts, to plow straight, to build an *izba*, and to plane boards. I also guided them in other problems of housekeeping. Every evening, before it was time for bed, I gathered them together in the schoolhouse and talked with them. Then I taught them prayers and sent them home.

I gave primers to the young people who came over from Alagan, Bashkaus, and Chodra. I taught them a little, praised their achievements, and sent them home. Nikolai Maizam was the best student. After he received a primer from me, he took it to every yurt and taught people a little. I also sent a teacher, Andrei Paryakin, to them and he went to the yurts and taught people from the small primer. When they had mastered a little, he came home. Those who had learned from the primer then taught others, and from then on, they began to teach each other. More than one hundred people learned in this way.

Once I went to the unbaptized who lived in a place called Kopysh. There were three yurts there. I went into one of them and saw in the first corner of the yurt, where they kept the chests of their belongings, there lay a primer. I asked, "Who is studying from this primer?" A young woman replied, "I have been studying it." I asked her to read, and she read very well. I wondered, "Who taught you to read?" "Nikolai Maizam taught me a little, and sometimes I ask people who already know about it to show me." I praised her, saying, "From this, because you have learned about the true God, you will become His servant." She answered, "That's why I am studying, so that I may become a servant of God." I said, "If you will firmly believe in God and be baptized, you will find great happiness, my daughter." After this I told her about God and His grace. The next year she was baptized and seventeen other people with her.

Another time I went to the upper reaches of the Bashkaus. There I baptized nine people; I went into the yurt belonging to the unbaptized pagan called Semeyen and talked with him about God. After I sat down, I looked into the main corner of the yurt, and there on the chest where they kept their valuables was a primer laid out on a plate. I asked, "Who among you is studying the primer?" Semeyen replied, "Nikolai Maizam, who works with you, gave it to our children. Now two of my sons are studying it, and one of them is getting on very well. At the moment they have gone to relations; if they were at home, you could test them."

While I was living at Cholyshman, I went every year in January to a meeting in Ulala of all the missionary workers. To reach Ulala I sailed along Lake Telets by boat. In winter this lake is very stormy both night and day, and the banks of the lake are so steep that it is impossible to travel along them on foot or horseback. Traveling across this stormy lake, I was saved on two occasions from disaster by God's grace.

Once, when we were returning from Ulala to Cholyshman across the lake, we made it only as far as Kugan. We could not go further because the water of the lake was very turbulent, so we sheltered in a cave for sixteen days. Our provisions became scarce, and we made them last by rationing them. Two of our fellow travelers wept. Seeing their tears, I encouraged and calmed them, but privately in the night I prayed hard for God's help. Our loving God heard our sinful prayers and did not allow us to die. On the seventeenth day the waters of the lake became more calm. We offered our prayers to God and set out in the boat. We spent one night on the journey and reached Cholyshman. After this for two days we drank tea and did not take anything else.

The next year, again on our return journey from Ulala to Cholyshman across the lake, we were obliged to spend twenty nights in the cave. We had enough provisions left for two days or maybe even less. My workers and the psalm singer who were with me were ready to burst into tears and, again, privately I offered my prayers. The next day, when I got up very early, I looked and saw that the lake had frozen in the night. I tried the ice near the bank and found that it was not strong enough to support a man, so we spent another night there. The next day I looked again, and the lake had frozen quite hard and the wind was blowing in the direction of Cholyshman. We climbed a hill, and I could see that the lake was frozen for twenty *versts* (twelve miles), but beyond that it was not frozen. As it was not possible for us to drag the boat as far as the unfrozen part, we made a sail from our tent and pushed the boat over the ice. It moved quite smoothly. As the wind grew stronger and stronger, the boat moved ever more quickly. We tried to hold it back by tying ropes to each side and, holding on to these ropes, we ran after the boat. When we reached the point where the water was no longer frozen, we rested and brewed some tea.

After our rest, we pushed the boat into the water of the lake and began to row. Suddenly, the wind increased, a mist gathered, and it started to snow. Then a strong storm began to blow on the lake, and the banks were no longer visible. We lost our way. In such a hopeless situation, we resigned ourselves to the will of God: we stopped rowing and allowed the boat to drift. When the wind seemed to drive our boat into thick ice, my fellow travelers shouted and wept. Some said, "The bottom of the Golden Lake will be the tomb where our bones will lie!" Saying this over and over again, they lay down in the bottom of the boat while the icy waves beat the boat from both sides. I was very afraid that the boat would soon break up, but above all the tears of my fellow travelers touched my heart and I was very concerned for them. At that moment before my eyes I saw St Nicholas, and I remembered that in former times when I was in trouble he had helped me on two occasions. I had given my promise to build a chapel on the bank of the lake in his honor. A long time had passed since those occasions, and I had not kept my promise.

When I remembered this, I began to pray to St Nicholas, vowing, "If we are now saved from death, then in your honor I will build a chapel on the bank of the lake." Meanwhile, our boat had moved over thirty *sazhen* (sixty yards) into the ice. With every gust of the wind, it went further. When I finished my prayers to St Nicholas, I noticed that the ice under the bow of the boat was beginning to divide in two. In front of the boat, the ice was clearing in a narrow strip as far as the point where there was no more ice. Ahead of us was an open path similar to a path through a thick forest. The ice was moving in an opposite direction to the wind. At the sight of such a miracle, my body was aglow. I was excited, my throat became tense, and I could not speak for a long time. Then I said to those who were traveling with me, "Get up and do not weep, for God has helped us." They stood up and quietly crossed themselves. I steered the boat into the part of the lake that was clear of ice, and it drifted in that direction. My workers took hold of the oars and wanted to start rowing, but I stopped them from doing that—I stopped them so that they would be able to see God's mercy to us. We did not row at all, but the boat itself moved as if we were rowing. It floated forward and moved out of the ice. We looked back: the pathway along which we had sailed had become once again part of the thick ice.

While we remained silently thoughtful, wondering in what direction we should row, the mist and snow in the space in front of us cleared, and the Beli bank of the lake appeared; we rowed in that direction. And so, by the mercy of God and with the help of St Nicholas, we safely reached the Beli bank of the lake. While we brewed some tea, no one said a single word. After a while I said, "Children, did you see that miracle?" The wife of one of my workers said, "If any of us here says that on this day he did not see God's miraculous help for us, then may God punish him." Others added, "Of course, we'll never forget this miracle for the rest of our lives."

After spending the night there, we set out the next day with God's help across the lake and reached Kyrsae, which is at the mouth of the Cholyshman. When we got home, we had a feeling of shame in our souls, as if we were guilty in some way. The next year, in fulfillment of my promise, I built a chapel by the lake in honor of St Nicholas. In it we built an altar. While we were building the chapel, all the pagans who lived nearby were converted to our faith and baptized. The most holy Macarios baptized some of them. There were more than a hundred baptized people there.

THE BAPTISM OF THE PEOPLE OF AK-KORYMSK

In Ak-Korymsk, about twenty *versts* (twelve miles) from where I lived, were more than ten yurts of unbaptized people. In the course of five years, I visited them often. I told them about God, about His kindness, and about His wonders. I related to them what had happened since Adam up to our times. They said, "We have heard such talk from the missionary Macarios, who spoke with us in Altai. Although he spoke the truth, nevertheless, we cannot reject our faith that we have inherited from our ancestors." They added, "We are afraid that if we were to be baptized and accept another faith, then Earth, Water, Holy Ulgen, and the spirits, to whom we are accustomed to offer sacrifice, will become angry with us and do us harm. And why do we need to be baptized anyway? Although the baptized people go to church and pray, they do not live any better than we do, nor are they richer." On hearing this I said to them, "Even the most hopeless and poorest of the baptized people possess wonderful incorruptible riches. For this reason, they are richer than even the richest of your people." Then I spoke to them of the incorruptible treasures of Heaven. Some of them began to waver in their minds and said, "Maybe some day we will be baptized, but at the moment we do not wish to." Seeing their doubts, I started to send the psalm singer, Yakov, to them on feast days, and he went to them and talked with them.

One year, on the third day of Pascha, I sent Yakov to talk with them. Within a day he sent me a letter: "The people here have for some reason begun to speak roughly with me; some of them will not listen to me at all. I want to return home." When I read this, I became very agitated and my heart burned within me. I rang the church bell. The newly baptized ran to me, both old and young, and asked in a very worried way what had happened. I said, "Take up the icons of the Savior, the Mother of God, and the saints, and set out up the Cholyshman to the baptized people who live in Koo. Spend the night there. I will come early in the morning. I will go round to all the homes of the newly baptized, and then we will sprinkle with holy water all the yurts that have become possessed by satanic fire so that we can put out these fires of the devil." In amazement the newly baptized asked, "Whose yurts are inflamed in this way?" I replied, "You will see when we get there."

A large number of people gathered, took up the holy icons, and set out to see the newly baptized at Koo. It was already nightfall when they arrived. I prayed to God and the next day set out early. On arrival I went round to all the yurts of the newly baptized and prayed with them. Then I gave the local elder of the place instructions to go to the pagans of Ak-Korymsk and give them a message: "You go to the inhabitants of Ak-Korymsk and speak to them openly; tell them that a priest has been sent to them who will tell them he has invisibly with him the King of kings, His Son, and His servants, who are coming to see them out of great concern for them. Let them all gather— old and young—on the banks of the Cholyshman and greet Him with respect. Let them not close the doors of their yurts to Him; otherwise, they will bring upon themselves the anger of the King's Son. Tell them that this is what the priest requested me to say." I asked the elder to repeat these words several times so that he would not forget. After giving him my blessing, I added, "Do not tell them that we have brought the icons here," and the elder set out.

After we had drunk tea, we took the icons and set out with them, singing "Christ Is Risen!" As we approached, we could see that the pagans of Ak-Korymsk, both old and young, were dressed in their best clothes and standing on the bank of the Cholyshman, waiting for us. When we got near, several of them fell to their knees. Seeing how they greeted us and showed such reverence, I wept to myself and remained for some time unable to say a word. Then after a while I said, "If you want to be happy, then show us the way to your yurts."

Chadan took us to his place first. The day was already drawing to a close, and it was about a *verst* to Chadan's yurt. While we walked there, singing as we went, all the unbaptized people walked at the side of the holy icons. When we arrived at Chadan's yurt, I said, "Where shall we put these icons for the night?" Chadan said, "It would not be right to put them in our yurt because we have pagan idols inside. Let them be put in the new wooden yurt for the night because it is clear inside. I will gather some felt, and cover the roof with it." Then he fetched the felt and covered the roof. We carried the holy icons into the yurt and left them there.

All the newly baptized people who had come to meet us went into the yurt, and with the greatest joy they looked at the holy icons. Showing the rest of the people the image of our Savior, I said to them, "Here is the image of Jesus Christ, Son of the King of kings. I told you before about Him and His goodness, but you ignored Him. He is invisibly present here and feels great pity for you, and He wishes that you should never be slaves of Satan but should become His children with the right to an inheritance from Him. He does not want you to fall into Hell and torments with the devil but rather that you should inherit everlasting joy in Heaven. God says, 'I am Your Lord, God,' and 'May you have no other gods but me.' He desires that you should not bow down to anything on earth or under the earth, for everything that is under the earth or on the earth is His creation. He wants to tell you, 'I am the Lord, your God, who has created everything. Come to me, all of you, and I will give you peace.' At a certain time the Lord, God, as He ascended from earth to Heaven, gave His disciples this command: 'Go into the whole world and teach the gospel to all of creation. Whoever believes and is baptized will be saved, and whoever does not believe will be condemned.' Following the Lord's command, I have been here many times to talk with you of the true God and the true faith, but you did not believe. Now God has come, as it were, Himself, in His icon. He Himself is invisibly with us." Then I told them about Jesus Christ again, beginning with His birth to the end of time.

They went out of the yurt and gathered together some distance from us in an open space, where they sat down in a circle and smoked and talked among themselves for about half an hour. Then they came over to us and said, "We all believe in God and wish to be baptized. When will you baptize us?" I said, "God is waiting for you all the time. Write down the names of your godfathers and godmothers and your own names." They wrote them down for me. The deacon and psalm singer, sitting separately, copied these down right up until midnight. In all there were thirty-eight names noted down. The next morning we taught them how to pray.

Meanwhile, I said to them, "Once there were forty people who came to believe in God in one day. One of them turned away from God and died straight afterward, but the thirty-nine others did not turn away from God, and wreaths of brightness descended from Heaven upon their heads." One of the pagans understood what

I was saying and added, "Out of forty people who had believed in God, one turned away, and I understand that the wreath sent to him by God returned to Heaven. So in order that the number should remain at forty, one man chose to believe in God. He truly began to believe in God instead of rejecting him." He thought some more and said, "If today forty people were to be baptized, then our numbers would be the same as that forty. But we are two people short." They all agreed, "It seems we are two persons short." They went into one of the yurts and brought out a girl, and a person who was ill came forward. Then they said, "Now, by God's mercy we have forty persons; also fourteen people have gone haymaking, and when they return they will be baptized."

We stayed the night there and in the morning baptized them all in the name of the Father, Son, and Holy Spirit. Carrying the holy icons, they accompanied us to the crossing of the Cholyshman, and we returned home singing on the way "Christ Is Risen from the Dead." Soon after I sent a psalm singer to them to teach them how to pray properly. It wasn't long before all the remaining people of the district were baptized.

About four times, I went to Cholyshman to the meeting of the missionaries. I would stay there for about a week and then go to see my Baiatsky Telyeut kinsmen. I would spend about a month there and then return to Cholyshman. Every time I went, I taught some pagans the faith and baptized them. Before I began to go there, the newly baptized lived among the pagans, and in this way it was like those people had two loyalties. It was much more difficult for me to teach these pagans than those who had been newly baptized. In the following years, it became easier for me to teach them because I went to see them during Lent. I persuaded them all to fast and then taught them the true faith, the Lord's commandments, and how to live in conformity with them. They said to me many times, "If only a church would be built here and a priest who could teach in our native language would be sent here, we would never waver and incline to evil." I said to them, "If you really mean that, then God will give you what you need, for God never refuses that which would be pleasing to Him." Their pleas reached God, and now they have a church of white stone and a priest who knows the Telyeut language. Glory be to God both now and ever!

My children! I am giving you these writings of mine describing my life as a testament that you may work harder for God than I worked for Him. I give you my blessing, which is upon you and your children from generation to generation in the centuries to come.

CHAPTER 4

Admonitions to My Children

TO MY CHILDREN AND
THEIR DESCENDANTS

May these words be a lesson for them;

May they be an exhortation from generation to generation.

Do not swear aggressively, hanging a millstone about your neck,

So that you may not fall upon evils that you will regret.

Do not get involved in quarrels with a knife in your hand,

And thus you will not weep when you have lost.

Guard your tongue carefully,

And you will not suffer from evil consequences.

Keep your tongue dumb,

And thus you will not be ashamed.

Do not give too much freedom to your tongue—
command it to be calm,
And you will not blink your eyes and weep.
Do not shout out a lot of words, and you will have
nothing to fear.
Do not slander anyone, and you will not become
sad and suffer.
Certainly never let impure words fall from your
lips,
And you will not be condemned to great suffering.
God does not like foul language,
And it will lead to such suffering as cannot be
avoided.

THE LONG ARM

Do not take too much from people,
And you will not fall into bitter troubles.
Do not reach out for too much,
And you will avoid torments in the future life.

Do not raise your hands to someone who offends
you,
And your arm will not suffer.
Do not let your hands become too greedy,
And people will not curse you.

Keep your hands to their work;
Compel them to be flexible.
A flexible hand is creative,
But one that is rigid will spoil things.
Perform acts of kindness with your hands,
And later this will give you joy.

A boastful hero does not prosper.
Do not be boastful of any heroic deeds,
And be restrained in quiet satisfaction.
A proud hero has to accept
That he loses his head and is lost.

One who boasts of his strength shortens his life
And will not see the light of the sun.
Do not vaunt your rank before those older than
you;
Do not boast of your superiority.

Be deferential to your elders;
Remember what you hear.
Be humble before a high official;
Do not be rude and evasive.

Be brief and precise before your chief,
Bow your head before him obediently,
Listen to his commands, and
Do not be pompous and rude.

Satisfy his desires and obey him.
Do not be proud and disobedient;
Do not be puffed up before your chief.
Do not sing the praises of your own knowledge.

Do not sing praises of yourself before the people;
Be kind and meek.
Do not make a show of your superiority before the
people,
And you will not be mocked and abused.

Do not pretend, and do not twist and turn like a
snake,
And you will not be wrongly slandered.
Do not flatter people with false generosity,
And you will not experience the misery of being
cursed.

Do not take pride in power or wealth;
Live as God commands.
Do not think of yourself as brainy,
And do not deliberately inflict great sufferings
upon yourself.
Do not think evil of any man,
And do not bring evil upon yourself.
He who thinks evil will be accursed
And go to Hell, to the fiery darkness.

MY CHILDREN!

My flesh and bones have become weaker;
I await the coming of the Divine Messenger.
My life has run its course;
I do not know whether I shall live longer, and
My powers have weakened.
Whether my days will continue, I know not.
My life's course has drawn to its close.
The words of my speech have been worn away;
The light of my eyes has darkened.
Many thoughts lie in my being, and
I have experienced much sadness.
My powers to relate tales are failing.
My vigor has begun to leave me;
I have become like a captive.
I am not immortal here.
Thy will be done, oh, God, my Creator.
His power can take me.
Do not ever depart from Him, I pray you:
God, my maker, do not leave me!
In thinking about my last days, I ask:
Cleanse me from my sins, oh, my God!

INDEX

agriculture, 39, 45, 47,
  69–70
Airy-Tash, 62
Akakii, Father,
  98, 109
Ak-Korymsk people,
  128–34
Ak-Umara (Obi)
  River, 2
aldachi (angel of death),
  53–54
Altai Book Publishing
  House, xvii
Ananin, Nikolai
  Ivanovich, 34–36
Anastasia, Nun, 88
Anastasios, Father,
  23, 28

Andreyevich, Mikhail,
  79–84
Arsenii, Father, 37–40
Ayu-Kechpes River, 68
Aza (demon), 50
Azh (mountain pass), 102

Bai-Ulgen. *See* Rich
  Ulgen
baptism, 6, 7, 10, 25–27,
  38, 42–43, 49–60,
  103–17, 128–34
Bedyurov, Brontoi Ya.,
  xviii
Belmont, Sofia, xv
Bible translation, xiv,
  30, 34
Buddhism, xiii

cassock, 120–21
Chernevy peoples, 91
Chernov, Kurman, 99
Chevalkov, Andrash, 1,
    15, 17, 29–30
Chevalkov, Andrian,
    10–11, 17, 29
Chevalkov, Grigorii, 27
Chevalkov, Kiprian, 10
Chevalkov, Konstantin, 91
Chevalkov, Maria, 1,
    77–78
Chevalkov, Matryona, 1,
    77–78
Chevalkov, Yelena, 1,
    77–78
Chichkan, Zaisan, 95–96
children, 27, 81, 110
China, 93–95, 96
Chinese *albyn*, 93, 94–95
Cholyshman, 53–54, 60–61,
    63–64, 121–2
Choposh, 115–7
"Christ is Risen!" (hymn),
    130, 133
Chui *zaisan*, 97, 99, 100
Chuisk elders, 95
Chyulyush River, 63

"Dark Kirgiz" (Kara
    Kazak), 2, 46
demon, 24–25, 50, 54.
    See also Aza
Denandel, xiv
Dmitrievich, Aleksei, 115

Erlik, 50, 66

Feast of Mikola (St Nich-
    olas), 7–9, 23, 37
Feast of Pascha, 47,
    118, 129
Feast of the Trinity, 19
fish(ing), 41, 47, 48, 60–61,
    67–68

Gorbachev, M. S., xvii

Herder, Johann Gottfried
    von, xiv
hieromonk, 82
High Altai region, xiii, xv,
    xvii–xi, 81

icons, 84–85, 122, 129–31
idols/charms, 38, 39–40,
    41, 65–66

interpreter, Mikhail
Chevalkov as,
33–76, 83, 91–103,
110
Ioann (Smolyanikov),
Father, 87, 107

Kaak, 107–9
Kadik, 104–5
Kalanak, 113–5
Kara Kazak. *See* "Dark
Kirgiz"
Karasuk people, 104
Karpovna, Domna, 84
Kochaev, Boris, 25–27
Komdoshsk, 69
Koninin, Alexander
Stephanovich,
119
Konshin, Afanasii, 3
Konshin, Yakov, 3–4
Korolkov, Ilya, 36
Kosh-Agach, 95–96,
99–102
Kulashev, Miron, 60
Kumandinsky peoples,
91
Kunkersky khan, 2

Kuzensk (pagan district),
69
Kyshtymsky clan, 1

Lake Telets, 43, 60–62, 68,
91, 124–27
Landysheva, Praskovia,
xv
language
of High Altai region,
xiii, 81
of Telyeut, 34
of Telyeut-Shorts
people, 38, 40
Lerkho, Govenor,
98–101
Linnaeus, xiv

Macarios (Andreyevich),
Father. *See*
Andreyevich,
Mikhail
Macarios (Glukharev),
Father, xiii–xv,
xviii, 5–7, 11–13,
17–27, 29–32
Macarios (Nevsky),
Father, 109–10

Maizam, Nikolai,
    122–123
Manicheanism, xiii
missionary work, xii,
    37–40, 65–66
Mother of God icon, 84,
    85, 122, 129
Motko, 104
Mundusov family, 1

Naurchakov, Mikhail, 36
Naurchakov, Osip, 18
Negritsky, Mikhail
    Petrovich, 22
Nestorianism, xiii
Nias, 53–54, 55

Obi. *See* Ak-Umara
Oirotsky khan, 2
Orozhok, 56–57
Orthodox Christianity,
    xii–xiii, xi
Orthodox Church, xii
Orthodox News, xvi

pagan ways, 1, 69–76, 74,
    89, 130, 132–34
Paryakin, Andrei, 122

Poryakin, Alexander, 31
prayer, 3–4, 16, 50–51,
    60–69, 85, 132
Prints, Andrei Gustavovich,
    91–103

Radlov, Vasilii Vasilevitch,
    x–xi, xvi
religion, xiii, xvii–xviii, 4,
    37–38
Rich Ulgen, 50, 54, 74–75,
    128
Russian *chashechniki*, 111
Russian emissary to
    China, 90–103
Russian Empire, High
    Altai region of, ix
Russian Orthodox
    Church, ix

sacrifices, 74–76, 115, 128
*Samples of the National
    Literatures of the
    Turkic Peoples*, xvi
Semeyen, 123
Shabalin, Yermolai, 31
shamanism, xiii, 4, 41,
    53–54, 55

Shchetinin, Andrei, 31
singing, 78–81
Smaragd, Father, 60
Soyonts peoples, 92
Stepan, Father, 34, 36, 52, 60, 78
Stepanovich, Yakov, 115
St Mitrofan, 18
St Nicholas, 60–69, 126
St Nicholas Day Feast. *See* Feast of Mikola
St Panteleimon, 122
studies, 78, 81, 122, 123
Surochakov, Pavel, 18, 23
Syuult people, 105–7

Tabakaev, Andrei, 21
Tabyshtu, 103
Taoism, xiii
Telyeut language, 34
Telyeutov clan, 2, 2n
Telyeut-Shorts people, 37–41
Theological Academy, Kostroma, xiv
Tiban, 53–60
Tirgesh Kergesh clan, 47–48, 54

Tiskenek, 111–2
Toolos people, 62, 63, 65–68, 92
translation, xvi, xvii, 18–19, 34, 81–82, 109–10, 117–18, 120 *See also* Bible translation
"The Truth Is All We Need" (hymn), 113
Tubints people, 43–46
Tugai (Uttu-Kai), 5
Tuzikov, Antonov, 94–95
Tuzikov, Luchshev, 94–95
Tyudyunekov, Pavel, 78–79
Tyurgeshck, 69
Tyurgets people, 61
Tyuuty family, 1

Ulala, 84–86, 88
Ulu, 42–43
Uttu-Kai. *See* Tugai

vaccinations, 103–4
Vasilii (godson), 107–8

Vasilii, Father, 16, 28, 60

Vasilievich, Ivan, 115, 116, 121

Vasilievich, Stepan, 18, 27

Vladimir, Father, 110

White Telyeutov clan, 1

White Tsar, 2, 93–95, 97, 100

wine, 57, 70, 72

women, 78, 81. *See also* women's monastery

women's monastery, 83–90

Yevdokia, Sister, 77, 78

Ynyrga people, 46–47, 104

Yurts people, 103–17

Yussk, 69

Zamyatin, Aleksei, 24–25